At Home

William Plomer

AT HOME

Memoirs

THE NOONDAY PRESS
New York

PRINTED IN GREAT BRITAIN

Contents

Preface

SOME years ago I published an autobiographical book, *Double Lives*. It had to do with my progenitors and my own early life, which was spent partly in Europe, partly in Africa, and partly in Asia. Readers who liked the book have often asked if there was to be a continuation of it. I now offer them this sequel, in which a young man of English origins and Afro-Asian conditionings returns to England in the late 1920s and settles there. It is inevitable that in writing of literary life in London in the 1930s I touch upon themes and personalities that have appeared in other memoirs, but unless I had thought I had something fresh to say I should not have begun to write this one.

T. S. Eliot has said that 'the progress of the artist is a continual extinction of personality'. The word 'extinction' seems a little strong, but in charting some of the circumstances in which I had my being after returning to England I have felt less interested in myself than in other persons, places, things, works of art, atmospheres, and ideas. In writing of them or of my own relation to some of them I have had to be elliptical, both for artistic and personal reasons.

Some passages in this book, paragraphs, or phrases, have appeared in print before, as parts of papers contributed to periodicals or miscellanies, or in one instance of a broadcast in the Home Service, and intended to serve as preliminary sketches for this work. I make grateful acknowledgments therefore to those editors or publishers who printed or commissioned them, particularly to John Lehmann, a tireless editor and a perennial encourager from the time when he joined my first publishers, the

Preface

Hogarth Press, through the years of *New Writing*, to the time of the *London Magazine*; to Cyril Connolly, as the editor of *Horizon*; to William Sansom, as editor of *Choice*, a miscellany published in 1946 by Progress Publishing; and to John Sutro, as editor of *Diversion: Twenty-Two Authors on the Lively Arts*, published by Max Parrish in 1950. I have also to thank Miss Harriet Grant for her unwearying and successful pursuit of a biographical detail, and Mr J. C. Longhurst for permission to quote from a letter contributed by him to the *Spectator* in 1957.

At Home

I

Through Siberia in a Trance

O N a fine, dry, starry night in the early spring of 1929 a Japanese steamer began to cast off from the quayside at Shimonoseki. She was the regular boat on her way to the port of Fusan in Korea. Clean and brightly lighted, she was quickly brought round with a wash and skirmish of water astern, and was about to head rapidly and purposefully westwards. The passengers were few. Only two were Europeans. They were strangers to each other, and I was one of them.

Standing alone on deck, I could feel through the soles of my feet the accelerated throbbing of the ship's engines, but my attention was fixed elsewhere. Like a bare stage brilliantly lighted, the receding quay was as clean as the deck, unencumbered with gear or goods, and now deserted except for one human figure. It was Morito Fukuzawa, a Japanese who had shared my life for a long time and had come all the way from Tokyo to see me off. From that lonely and lessening form under the arc-lamps there presently came, in a voice made strong by emotion and enlarged in the empty night by the high roof above him which acted as a sounding-board, the Japanese valediction, that forlorn word 'Sayonara!' He uttered it four times, at what seemed long intervals, and four times over the calm sea I called back those four sad syllables. The last time I was surprised by the volume of my own voice, but I knew that by the time the word reached him it would be faint, ghostly, final. Long after Shimonoseki was out of sight I seemed to hear him still.

It was not an easy parting. We had lived on terms of close friendship under the same roof and in the Japanese style, and had travelled about the country together, understanding one another perhaps as nearly as the barriers of tradition, race, language, and education would allow. I cannot judge for which of us the parting was less easy. It might have been harder later. At this time we were both young. We had our separate destinies, and possibly I was the more fortunate of the two: I seemed more hopeful by nature, freer, more forward-looking. But he had a kind of wisdom, not unmixed with disillusionment and resignation, which was not mine. He also had the advantage of remaining on the soil to which he belonged and knew he belonged, whereas my young allegiances had been dispersed between Europe, Africa, and Asia.

From that moment I went into a kind of trance. It was not simply because I missed my familiar companion and had torn myself from the life in Japan I had grown accustomed to. It was also a matter of disposition. Those who are not bent upon what is called 'getting on' fall easily into trances, into a mood that may last through a lifetime of semi-indifference, of habit fitting as comfortably as an old overcoat, of dreamy resignation: and such a state, though its causes are no doubt partly physical, is by no means incompatible with activity of body or mind. Contributory to my trance was an enormous ignorance — of politics, economics, languages, geography — which made it impossible to see things, places, and people in proper perspective.

The next morning, when the express began rushing northward through Korea, unfamiliar scenes, caught in glimpses, began to succeed one another too rapidly to be apprehended, and fragments of literature, geography, and history eddied through my mind like straws in a wind-tunnel. Sudden perceptions of contrast, like unexpected juxtapositions of sound in a smooth piece of music, often startled me out of my trance. In the new and well-equipped train Japanese businessmen in white collars, black coats and striped trousers sat about smoking, reading newspapers, and talking about stocks and shares; outside it the bare mountains of Asia, rocky and remote in the pale sunshine, glided past in silence, as if floating or changing places according to some predetermined manœuvre, and beneath them from time to time could be seen stately Korean gentlemen of leisure wearing full white robes and tiny top-hats of black gauze tied with ribbons under the chin, *as if nothing had happened*— as if there was no train, no line, no Japanese expansion, no next war germinating. The whole of our time — if by our time we mean the whole period since the Industrial Revolution — has abounded in such contrasts between formal survivals from the long ages of what may be called the Hand-Made and manifestations of what is called progress. The sentimental romanticism of the nineteenth century, with its feeble or heartfelt attempts to catch and hold the vanishing 'picturesque', its hankerings for what Tennyson's brother Charles called 'old ruralities', its cries of 'Verweile doch, du bist so schön!' is not dead yet.

As a child I had seen Chinamen wearing pigtails; at Mukden I saw in the street a richly dressed Chinese woman tottering along on tiny bound feet, a belated martyr to an uncommonly perverse fashion. I supposed it was the mingled appearance of helplessness and affectation which these broken, crippled, trotter-like feet gave to the gait that had caused them to be thought beautiful. Possibly for the male the sexual attraction lay in the certainty that, if pursued, no woman with such feet could run away. But behind this

13

woman loomed smoking factory chimneys. On their black stilts the Satanic mills were after her. They would soon overtake her. She would never be seen again.

While blue-shadowed snow still lay in shady places, the early spring sun was already bright on the biscuit-coloured plains of Manchuria, and those blue stains were repeated in the people's clothes, often faded or washed out to a smoky or chalky turquoise. Whole tracts of fawn-coloured country opened out from the train like fans decorated with little knots or dots of blue that were peasants at work. But at Harbin the sky was overcast, and for the first time I had the feeling of being in Russia—not Bolshevik Russia, not Czarist Russia, but a sort of Russian no-man's-land in some unwritten novel. From the uncomfortable glitter of fixed bayonets at the station I stepped into the street and saw that it was not Russia: a dignified elderly Chinese, dressed in black, was giving money to a flaxen-haired young Russian beggar standing in the gutter. In some ways Harbin did look like a Russian provincial town. The presence there of many White Russian emigrés fostered the illusion. Other displaced persons of many varieties gave it at the same time a certain cosmopolitanism: there was a Viennese restaurateur who said he made the best coffee in Asia and was affably fluent in several languages. Extremes of poverty and patches of luxury were in evidence, and over everything hung an atmosphere of suspense and uncertainty. There were indications of intrigue, of the sinister and the corrupt. In the daytime the streets were drab and lethargic, but late in the afternoon the town yawned and stretched itself. Lights were turned on, faces were painted, and the febrile night-life of a lonely city, without morale and with the most precarious outlook, began to throb.

I paid a morning call on Madame S., half Russian and half

French, to whom I had undertaken to convey a message. I found her in what could only have been called a boudoir, the sort of room in which a ham actress might have delighted twenty years earlier. It was full of lacy hangings, braided trimmings, and crowded bibelots—so full that one could scarcely move without ducking or sidling. The draped shawls, framed photographs, and hanging yataghans seemed to have huddled together for safety, as if inanimate things too were driven by some herd-instinct to resist change by hiding from it. But with joy I recognized the samovar: it called up for me the enchanted world of Russian fiction, which I can honestly say had meant much more to me than English fiction. I hoped the denizen of the apartment would be like somebody out of Dostoievsky, voluble, and in a spiritual ferment. She proved to be much more like a Chekhov character. Her talk was largely about how she had set out for Paris after the Russian Revolution, had got as far as Harbin, where she had found herself saddled with various responsibilities and tethered by various frustrations, and was still bound for Paris—if only she could get her husband to leave Harbin. This was already more than ten years after the Revolution. Perhaps she is still there, scanty-haired, toothless, bent double among the fringed anti-macassars and darkening icons, still hoping, still clasping her hands, and quavering in a rapturous whisper, 'Ah, Paris!'—her husband, perhaps, having collaborated or pretended to collaborate with the Japanese, the Japanese puppet regime, Soviet agents, White Russian refugees, Nationalist Chinese, Communist Chinese, in turn, or all at once, in order not to leave Harbin. But I doubt if she dresses now as she was dressed when the bead curtains clashed apart and she stepped forward to greet me. The fashions of those days often lent even a chaste woman a look of wickedness—but the wickedness of a precocious and delinquent schoolgirl. There was something furtive and adolescent about those brimless beehive hats that all but hid the eyes; there was something of the gym-tunic about those short dresses, cut loose and square, with the waistline round the pelvis, and the skirt ending at the knees. Ah, Madame S., your Paris was behind your mirror! It was not bound feet that were your trouble or your fascination, but the bound psyche of the displaced person.

One afternoon I was taken to a resort of pleasure which was evidently not at its best in the daytime, and which did not compare favourably with the refinements of the same sort of establishments in Japan. My companion and I were shown into a large, unaired parlour with sleazy red-plush divans round the walls, on which were gaudy frescoes of pairs of heroic sunburnt lovers, more than lifesize, in a fancifully tropical setting. There was a stale miasma of last night's fumes of tobacco and vodka, and a general air of seedy hangover. The girls were asleep or resting, but one or two were up and about. We went upstairs, where the air was better, drank Kirin beer, and tried to make conversation. A young Russian girl, a mousy blonde of about seventeen, drew my attention to a gaudy postcard pinned to the wall. It must have come from Natal and showed a handsome Zulu. The consequences of being oneself are unpredictable: that he should have become this girl's pin-up man could hardly have been imagined. From the window I could see a tough-looking Chinese manservant sweeping the yard; above and beyond him, over the roofs, the wide and mournful river Sungari, like a vast width of dark grey silk, was being endlessly unrolled between its snowy banks, for ever and ever. There was no wind, the air was chill and dry, and lights were beginning to be turned on for the town's awakening to another night of night-life. I felt that I was seeing life, but I would rather have seen it gayer.

Through Siberia in a Trance

It was time to take the Chinese Eastern Railway through the Great Khingan Mountains and over the Barya steppe to the Siberian border. Somnambulistic, I was gently guided by a fellow traveller, an amiable Czech. If he did not break the trance, he let some light of consciousness in. It was a valuable service, yet I can't even remember his name: such is the gratitude of the entranced. He spoke fluent Russian and English, and willingly interpreted for me when we conversed with Russians. He had been here ten years earlier, in the Czech legion that had fought, I believe under Koltchak, the Bolsheviks. He was without prejudice against them, and was anxious to see what they had done and were doing to make a new Russia. From the train we looked out over dune-like wastes of a most forbidding loneliness to the sunless Gobi Desert. At Manchuli, in those days a one-horse, one-storeyed frontier township, we had a drink of kvass, and when, in the slushy street, we stopped to talk to a much-wrapped-up and bearded old man who smelt stronger and cheesier than anybody I ever met, I knew that I had entered the world of Gorki, where distances were in versts, payments in kopecks, and souls naked and tormented. So real had Russia been made to me by the Russian writers I had read in translation that it was impossible to feel like a stranger.

We found ourselves enclosed for the journey in an ancient wagon-lit decorated in the art nouveau style with fancy woodwork and figured dark-blue velvet. The atmosphere was stale, so I made as if to open a window. In my ignorance I did not know that for nine months of the year it was forbidden to open the windows because cold air would rush in, and for the remaining months it was ordered that they were to be kept shut because of the dust. There was a dining car, more remarkable for its vodka and excellent macaroons than for lavish meals, and we had been warned to supplement our diet by buying food from the peasants at wayside stations. So we did. We bought all sorts of things, the most notable and lasting of which was a cold roast goose, tender in spite of its ostrich-like dimensions. We also bought honey enclosed in a container made of a hollowed-out section of a young birch-tree. This rustic receptacle proved not wholly satisfactory. When our backs were turned, honey exuded into our pyjamas and socks, and when we tidied our hair we found quite a new meaning for the phrase 'honey in the comb'. At the rare stations boiling water was on tap, and the overcoated passengers queued with teapots: my Czech, like a wise virgin, had provided us with one before leaving Harbin.

The next excitement was Lake Baikal. One morning there were mountains, wooded mountains, some of them six or seven thousand feet high. Handsome conifers towered above the train, which presently began running in and out of short tunnels round the southern edge of the lake. Baikal, on which there were small distant boats, extended there below us in the sun, not a lake but an inland sea more than three hundred miles long. It was like a secret sea, because one had never thought about it. Like all this hardly imaginable northern world it had only the vaguest place in one's conception of the world as a whole. Siberia, even on a modern map, was much like some terra incognita on an ancient map, and marked similarly with place names outlandish and few — Ushumun, Amazar, Sungor, Turuchansk — but with this difference, that through it ran this thread, this clue, this nexus of railway, leading the traveller through steppe and tundra and taiga to Europe. And now the clue had brought us to Baikal, the deepest lake in the world. It was said to be full of delectable fish, and in a capitalist world would soon have become a millionaire's playground. It was restful not to see vulgarians in big sports cars but Mongol fishermen in fur caps minding their own business in a vast silence. Originally, it was said, the Trans-Siberian railway stopped abruptly at the western shore and began again on the eastern, the trains being ferried across in the summer and in the winter driven over rails laid on the ice, until one winter the ice gave way and a train was drowned. I doubt if the story is true, but it can only have been at a great expense of time, money, and labour that the railway was taken round the southern shore and tunnel after tunnel driven through the mountain buttresses.

Beyond Irkutsk the ice was breaking up in a rapidly flowing river of crystalline water rushing eastwards. Chunks and slabs of ice tilted, swam, or piled up against obstructions, and showed their emerald and sapphire tints to the whitish but strengthening afternoon sun; and on the further bank groves of young silver birch trees, quite leafless still, gleamed and trembled as if with a consciousness of returning sap. By now we were getting used to the vastly spaced-out stations, where we left the train once or twice a day to buy food, make tea, and stroll about in the cold, pure air. When one left the train the silence struck the ear like a blow, and then each casual sound—the panting of the engine, the snatches of dialogue, the barking of a dog or crowing of a cock—was enlarged into a monstrous nearness and exactness. The sensation of space, silence, and emptiness I had known in Africa, but never quite this feeling of immensity. I had read that Russia's Arctic coastline extended to something like seventeen thousand miles, and at Irkutsk we were still far more than a thousand miles from the Arctic Ocean. To someone coming from the swarming warrens of Tokyo and bound for the drab agglomerations of London the pure and silent Siberian air was like a new and unknown element, and when one saw some solitary man driving off in a troika, or two women with kerchiefs on their heads and wearing big felt boots trudging away into a landscape at times so featureless that it seemed nothing but a perpetual motion of slowly receding horizons, their journeys seemed acts of courage. The stations and towns at long intervals — Chita, Krasnoyarsk, Novosibirsk, Omsk — had been witnesses of war and revolution, and before that of enforced exile: in their past their future was implicit, of growth and change. Certain buildings put up in Czarist days, solid and well-proportioned under their light-coloured stucco, owed their style to Italian influences in Russia in the eighteenth and early nineteenth centuries. They now wore Bolshevik emblems, stars and sickles and hammers. There were still traces to be seen of the fighting after the Revolution, and already there were signs of that huge expansion of strength to which the Revolution gave the first great impetus and which has since transformed many places in Siberia.

Among the passengers was a lean, lone American who only travelled part of the way with us. Something between a prospector and a mining engineer, he seemed to be more ignorant of Siberia and the Russian language than was right for a prospective resident. He was an ingenuous, credulous, boyish man, and was very anxious to know what was before him when he left the railway to travel by cart or sleigh, or both, to a goldfield in the far north. His male fellow passengers — and among us was a cynical young Frenchman — were tempted to tell him tall stories. Like heartless, teasing boys we competed to see how much we could make him swallow. We told him gravely of myriads of wolves and bears, aggressive and perpetually hungry, man-eaters all. At this time of year, we said, only a small percentage of northward-bound travellers could expect to get through unscathed. If they did get through they would soon be tormented by three months of extreme heat and perpetual daylight. Sleep would in any case be impossible owing to the mosquitoes. Mosquito nets and insecticides, we explained, were not merely unobtainable but unknown, and the insects, though fortunately not malarial and admittedly smaller than wolves and bears, surpassed them in numbers and in appetite for human blood. Owing to the high intake of icecream in the United States, we said, mosquitoes were known to be particularly partial to the blood of Americans. With the first breath of autumn, we went on, the temperature fell abruptly —so abruptly that the mercury had been known to fall out of thermometers not stoutly constructed; by mid-winter the cold was so intense that speech became impossible—it froze on being uttered and fell clattering to the ground. The winter diet was little varied; tallow was the mainstay, because it was an antidote to cold; there was also black bread, soggy and coarse, with a high proportion of the roughest roughage. Radio and newspapers were unknown. And what, he asked, were the people like? What did they do in their spare time? Exchanging resigned looks and shrugging our shoulders, we competed in gravely inventing deplorable domestic manners and embarrassing sexual customs, with which he would of course have to conform. His eyes grew big with apprehension and he seemed paler under his weathered skin. His relief when we managed to persuade him, before he left, that we had been kidding him all the time was a pleasure to watch. Or was he perhaps a splendid actor, kidding us that we were kidding him? I think not. Innocence is so rare that it is not easily mistakable.

After the American had left us we were joined by another engineer, a Russian from Semipalatinsk, where he had been working on the building of the Turksib railway. He was in his thirties, animated, voluble, shrewd and humorous, with a refined face and a smart embroidered blouse. Thanks to my Czech companion's interpreting I was able to carry on long conversations with this agreeable man, the first real Bolshevik I had met. It was obvious that he enjoyed life, because he was full of confidence and hope in his own and his country's future He did not preach, he did not even talk politics, he exulted. Every now and then he broke into song, and if there had been room I suppose he would have danced. More than once I thought of the exiled girl in the brothel at Harbin. I felt that she might have been happier in Semipalatinsk.

Night after night, day after day, Siberia was rolling past the windows, not monotonous and by no means always bleak. There were fine rolling green steppes, and birch forests, and prairies where the soil looked fat and fertile. The frozen marshes of the taiga came nearer to the Siberia one had imagined, a Siberia of exiles and misery. The considerable town of Sverdlovsk, formerly Ekaterinburg, was under snow when we reached it, beneath a dark grey sky. It was of a forbidding aspect, the more so because one knew it to be the place where the Czar Nicholas II and his family had been done to death. The public rooms of the station were frowsty and crowded with people who sat or lay about the floor with bundles of possessions, some asleep, some lethargic. They looked as if they had been there a long time, waiting without hope for some long overdue train, and with nowhere else to go. There was a strong smell of old clothes and dill pickles. I stood at a window looking at the town in the leaden afternoon: it seemed lifeless, as if under a curse.

The journey across Siberia itself had taken nine days and nights: it was the longest train journey in the world. As we approached the Urals and European Russia we seemed to be returning to winter. The whole country was deeper in snow under a dark sky. A derailment somewhere ahead caused us to be held up for the best part of a day at a small station on the way to Kazan. Near the station was a village where it was apparently market day. The peasants came down to the station and took much interest in us passengers. In spite of language difficulties there was cheerful fraternization. My Czech companion, unhindered by these difficulties, persuaded a friendly moujik to take us for a ride in a horse-drawn sleigh. We went off at a tremendous pace, and it was almost disappointing to see that the train was still in the station when we got back. The interlude was one of those delightful accidents of travel which bring one for a moment much nearer to what is strange.

As the landscape became flatter and slightly more populous and one saw ancient-looking villages with clusters of houses and clumps of trees round churches with gilt, onion-shaped domes, and small wooden manor houses with pillared porticos, I realized how clearly my ideas about Russia had been formed by Gogol, Tolstoy, Dostoievsky, Aksakov, Turgeniev, Chekhov, Gorki, and Bunin—so formed that I seemed to *recognize* what I saw, as if returning from a long absence. Even in Moscow itself, though awed and excited, I strangely did not feel like a stranger. It was a place where I had often lived and suffered vicariously, and it was haunted by characters whom I felt I had known, whom I almost felt I had *been*. Such is the power of literature.

Not being politically minded and not well informed about the Revolution, I bought in Moscow a copy of *Ten Days That Shook The World*, and found it dull and almost unreadable, so I gave myself up to enjoying the visual splendour of the city so far as possible (we were not allowed into the Kremlin) and the human contacts my Czech companion was able to arrange. We went one evening to the Bolshoi Theatre to see a popular spectacle called *The Red Poppy*. The splendid interior, formerly a setting for jewels, uniforms, and grandes toilettes, was now filled with an audience in working clothes, homely, serious, respectable-looking people, conventional-looking, too, in a lower middle class, yes, a bourgeois, sort of way—though in the former Imperial box a woman with a kerchief over her hair gnawed an apple until the curtain went up. The scene was laid in Shanghai. The plot was simple, but developed by a battalion of performers, ballets, choruses, spectacular lighting, and loud music. An apparently English naval officer, abetted by a few Chinese, tried to induce a Chinese courtesan to offer poisoned wine to his rival, the commanding officer of a Soviet ship. She refused, and was murdered. On her deathbed she kissed a red flower previously given her by the Russian officer, and then, although in extremis, managed to preach a revolutionary homily to a group of Chinese children. A crimson map of China appeared in mid-air, and the curtain came down in a perfect frenzy, to which both audience and orchestra contributed their loudest.

The walls of the Kremlin reflected in the river, the Red Square, the views over rooftops of solid early nineteenth century buildings, the absence of traffic and advertisement, the ancient droshkies, the encrusted ecclesiastical splendours, the evidences of religious feeling and of poverty, the sad, ancient, barbaric atmosphere, the sensation of grandeur, of the world's most enormous hinterland behind this muffled, mysterious, tragic town, the underlying pulse of new power and purpose, little outwardly evident at that time—all this made an overwhelming impression of being in one of the nerve centres of history.

The museums seemed to be of two kinds, those where remains of past cultures were preserved and those which celebrated the Revolution. They were then being much used to indoctrinate the young, who could be seen going round in eager squads at any time of the day and being lectured to on the usual lines. At the

Through Siberia in a Trance

Tretiakov Gallery there were some unpleasant realistic pictures of the misdeeds of the Czars. Before a large canvas showing Ivan the Terrible immediately after the act of killing his own son a group of silent people stood staring as in the Middle Ages people might have looked at a cautionary picture of Hell. At the Historical Museum, in a room devoted to illustrations of life in the early nineteenth century I came across a copybook used in those days by a young nobleman. He had been required to write out the following sentence in Russian, French, and English:

The sense of Honour is of so delicate a nature that it is only met with in Minds that are naturally Noble or in such as have been cultivated by good Examples or a refined Education.

While I was reading this, a class of some forty adolescent boys and girls were being given a purposeful lecture by a buxom young instructress, who was showing them a series of prints depicting the various corporal punishments used in the wicked old Czarist days upon prisoners in Siberia. For all I know, she may have been saying that there would never be any more prisoners sent to Siberia.

As I sat down to dinner that night in the Grand Hotel I unfolded a table napkin of the finest linen, woven with the crown and monogram of the Czar Nicholas II, and out of it ran a cockroach.

2

Mrs Fernandez and Dr Pood

To cross the frontier between Soviet Russia and Poland was in those days to go from shabbiness and gloom to neatness and order. The change was immediately noticeable. Fields, gardens, and houses were well cared for; the inhabitants had a more upright bearing, more open faces; the customs officials and railwaymen were spruce and civil. It would be too easy to say that to cross this frontier was to cross from Asia into Europe. Frontiers are false, inconstant things. This one no more divided Europe from Asia than do the Ural Mountains. There is no hard and fast barrier between Europe and Asia, and Europeans have lost the right—if they ever had the right—to regard barbarism as something that begins where Europe, or European civilization, has its ostensible boundaries. If there is one thing clear to any thinking person who has survived the first half of this century it is that there are no limits to human violence and cruelty.

To speak of Warsaw as it was then is to try and look back through a chaos of cruelty and suffering to a city whose civilization seemed balanced and comprehensible, though it was neither perfect nor secure. The Roman Catholic religion, the survival of a landowning class, the links with France, and the elegant eighteenth-century architecture all contributed to the grace and order of the city. The pleasure of perceiving something of its quality I owe to my old schoolfellow, Darsie Gillie, at present the Paris correspondent of the *Manchester Guardian*. He was then living in Warsaw. Even as a boy at Rugby he had shown a more than ordinary appetite for knowledge and power of assimilating and applying it. I forget how long he had been in Poland but he seemed to have completely mastered the language, and I remember the cheerful firmness with which he corrected some fault of usage or pronunciation made by an imperfectly educated Pole. He also showed great kindness in taking me about, showing me the sights, and introducing me to various forms of Polish life. The Lazienki Palace, the Jewish quarter, a cabaret, a literary salon, the best place to drink mead or borsch, and patience with an ignoramus—he displayed them all.

By way of Berlin, to which I was to return a year later, I came at last to Ostend. The winter of 1928–9 had been more than usually severe, and although it was, I think, already April and the sun was shining, a wind which seemed to have followed me from Siberia did not make the crossing to Dover something to look forward to. It was still early in the day, and the prospective passengers, congregated in the open air just before embarkation, were not in a jovial mood. We were a mixed lot, by no means all English, and among us was a tall Englishwoman with a figure like a cricket bat—straight, narrow, flat in front and only slightly convex at the back. Her tweeds, her long shanks and feet, her managing nose, and her big front teeth would have made her perfect raw material for some virulent German or French cartoonist of the Boer War period. Her supercilious yet carrying voice was in keeping. To borrow a phrase of my brother's, it could only have been evolved 'behind the Tweed Curtain'. It had in it more than a hint of arrogance, as if its function was to convey that her position in life was so assured—racially, socially and economically—that she had no need to worry about her want of feminine grace. It was the kind of voice that helps to destroy empires: no doubt something like it was once heard in Byzantium.

The owner of the voice might fairly have been classified as an upper middle class ungentlewoman. After glancing round at the wind-bitten, bluish, resigned faces of the other passengers, she said to her male companion (possibly a son or nephew) in an ineffably condescending drawl, pitching her voice so that we could all hear her:

'Everybody has an expression as if they were just going to take the first fence.'

This was perhaps her idea of a bon mot. It was in its way true, and issuing from some jolly, saddle-bashing riding mistress would have been harmless enough. It did not seem harmless to me. It seemed as if she wanted us all to know that the language of the hunting field was natural to her, and that if it was not natural to us, so much the worse for us, whatever we were.

Anybody may make some casual remark, in keeping with his nature and without harmful intention yet liable to make a bad impression when overheard. The bad impression made upon me by this particular remark has as much to do with me as with its utterer. Being young, I was (I hope) suitably intolerant, but she had struck more of a chill into me than the east wind. I must try and explain why.

One of the effects of having left England when very young and of having been long absent was that although I came back with many pleasant memories of English people, places, and things, I came back as a displaced person. Displacement had enabled me to understand, as I could not otherwise have understood, something of the strangeness a foreigner approaching England for the first time might feel, especially if he lacked the comfortable backing of a settled political and social background, a substantial capital, and secure prospects. Such a foreigner, even if unprejudiced, might feel some apprehension about the English character and about some of the traits he might have heard attributed to it. I for my part harboured disagreeable memories of a certain English attitude to life against which I had from early childhood been in rebellion. And now that I had sometimes seen this attitude disagreeably and one might almost say indecently exposed abroad, to the detriment of our national reputation, I was even more sensitive to it and even less ready to make allowances for it.

As a child I had perceived though I could not then have defined this attitude. Having been a boy in the period called Edwardian, I am now of the opinion that it might almost as well be called Late Victorian, and that up to the year 1914 there was no very significant change in English ways of life and thought. If the adults I liked least as a child were complacent, insular, and hypocritical, their habits of mind had certainly been made possible by their having been born and brought up in the second half of the nineteenth century. Some of them were concerned, among other things and other people, with bringing me up, and I saw them as large as life and quite as ugly. Their religion did not seem to have warmed their hearts; their principles seemed too narrow and rigid; their culture, though grounded on the classics, was of a deplorable thinness and poverty; their conventionality was unquestioning; they were dominated by materialism, and their imaginations had atrophied under the sheer weight of national, social, family, and personal self-satisfaction. Any but athletic pleasures enjoyed by other people or by the young were liable to incur their disapproval and vindictiveness, and their ignorance of the non-British peoples of the world was more than tinged with contempt. In the lady of the first fence I had recognized instantly a female of the species. Each of us might have tickets to London, but my destination was quite different from hers. Her London would have been more alien to my temperament than some of the remote places I had known, than Hluhluwe or Noboribetsu.

What on earth I seemed like when I returned to England I find it hard to imagine. I think I retained for some time the formal and I suppose defensive manner to which I had become accustomed when living with the Japanese. I may also have brought with me some traces, still adhering, of protective colouring.

'You've come back with a golden face,' my mother said as soon as she saw me.

Going about without a hat in Japan may have given my naturally anything but sallow skin a tinge of the local complexion. My eyes were not slanted 'at ten to two', as they say, nor had they developed the epicanthic fold, but they were sometimes as surprised at what they saw as Japanese eyes might have been. I remember for instance noticing with astonishment how well dressed the younger English working men and girls were. They did not seem to be wearing working clothes at all. Was England now becoming a standardized lower middle class nation, with the rich being impoverished at one extreme and the poor enriched at the other? As a child I had seen glimpses, through loopholes in the solid ramparts of Late Victorian comfort that protected me, of ragged tramps, barefooted urchins, and drunken viragos. I saw none now.

I continued my habit of not wearing a hat. It was then exceptional, even eccentric. Some allusion being made to it at a luncheon party in London, an amiable man next to me said, 'Oh, but don't you think it looks a little *shoppy* to go about without a hat?' I was puzzled by this, and asked what he meant. He explained that he meant '*like a shop assistant*'. I said it had not occurred to me, and I should not really much mind if I *were* mistaken for a shop assistant. He died a year or two later of pneumonia brought on in winter at his wife's funeral. Instead of standing bareheaded by the grave he would have been wiser not to have taken off his hat. It may have been necessary to suffer in order to appear respectful, but death was a severe penalty for having taken the appalling risk of looking like a shop assistant.

I cannot say I was deeply interested in my own appearance, but I remember my old friend the painter H. E. du Plessis said at this time that I looked like 'a mixture of Puck and Buddha', so I suppose my evident but unconsciously acquired Eastern aspect was enlivened by gleams of Western playfulness. I had already learnt that many people expect a writer to look like the image they have formed of him in their own minds. I had hardly set foot in England before somebody or other exclaimed, 'Oh, but you don't look in the least like your books!' or 'You don't look at all as I had imagined you!' Several times since then strangers have come up to me and begun a conversation, mistaking me for a doctor — each time a different doctor. A serious-looking man in a club once took my hand in his and told me how glad he was to hear of my new appointment at Bart's. A year or two later an eagerly friendly refugee couple, perhaps Austrian, clung to me in the street, beaming and exclaiming, 'Ach, sind sie wirklich Doktor Gruber?' And I have actually been congratulated on my successful treatment of a difficult case of hydrocele. I have thought these mistakes gratifying, because a doctor may be expected to have some insight into human nature and some powers of diagnosis, prognosis, and analysis.

To have called myself a displaced person is perhaps to appear to angle for sympathy. It would be more exact to call myself a repatriated person. My parents had returned for good from South

At Home

Africa and I went to spend the summer with them in their house, which was far enough from London for nightingales to be heard in the garden, but not too far to prevent my dining in London and returning home by a late train. I write 'their house', not 'their home', because they were never long enough in one place for it to be regarded as a home, either by them or their children. But their kindness, and the trouble they took to make me *feel* at home, provided perfect conditions in which to write. I was working at my second novel, and when it was finished I moved to London. What were my motives? First, the need to function as a writer, and to exercise and try to develop whatever talent I might possess, in what seemed the best environment. Next, curiosity about people and about London itself, and the impetus to unlock a London of one's own. Those main motives are, I believe, in the truthful order of precedence.

Looking back, I am mildly surprised at my unworldliness, but not ashamed of it. I had at that time no responsibility for contributing to the support of others, no intention of marrying, and almost no interest in trying to make more money than was needful to keep myself clothed, fed, warm, and clean, and to perform such small acts of charity or present-giving and make such modest returns of hospitality as might be possible for an indigent bachelor. I had no wish to impress anybody with my manner of living. I felt no need to own or use many of the things that many people found indispensable, like a telephone, a car, or a club, perhaps because I had lived quite happily without them elsewhere. I had not the faintest ambition to write best sellers. I should never have thought that my cast of mind was at all fitted to engage the interest of a large public. Nor was I set on any particular literary form. I wished to write prose or verse in various forms, as the spirit moved me, and, I hoped, in such a way that everything I wrote would be part of a gradually evolving interpretation of life in terms of my own art. As for the business of making a living, I have never been pushful, and would not have dreamed of soliciting any kind of favour or help from the eminent or the rich, from relations or friends, or of asking for any kind of job. Such ambition as I had lay entirely in the twin spheres of literature and of personal relationships. Both are impossible without leisure. As J. B. Yeats, the father of the poet, said in one of his letters: 'A society of *poor* gentlemen upon whose hands time lies heavy is absolutely necessary to art and literature.'

My family had had associations with London for at least four centuries, and I myself had often stayed there as a child. Now, at twenty-five, I entered it alone.

The first question was whereabouts I was going to live. It would not have occurred to me to settle in Bloomsbury. I was not drawn to Chelsea, which I knew of old, and it seemed now to have a new, floating population of well-to-do culture vultures. Kensington was too sober, Mayfair too smart; and when I saw in some paper an advertisement of 'chambers near Hyde Park' I followed it up.

I envisaged one of those quiet, clean, comfortable, old-fashioned establishments not far from the Marble Arch, kept by some urbane ex-butler whose wife had been a housekeeper or a lady's maid, the sort of house in which before 1914 my parents had sometimes taken rooms on visits to London. I was quite mistaken. Imagination could hardly have allowed for what lay in hiding beyond that advertisement.

The house was in Bayswater, to which I was not at all disinclined. My grandfather, while still serving in India, had taken a house for his wife and children in Stanhope Street in the 1860s. My parents had been married at St John's Church in 1901. And

At Home

in 1918 I had tottered light-headedly out of a Bayswater nursing home after recovering from the Spanish influenza. I liked the quarter. It was quiet and near central London, and in 1929 not gloomy and decayed as it became later. The afterglow of Victorian prosperity had not yet wholly faded and I liked the Victorian atmosphere and architecture, not because I had any sentimental hankering for the past but because I have always taken a great interest in the social history of the nineteenth century. As soon as I saw the house containing my prospective 'chambers' I was pleased by its looks. There was nothing mournful or faded about it. Perhaps built in the 1850s, it was villa-like, not tall and gaunt but with a cheerful light stucco façade, some pretty leafage behind the massive iron gate and railings, a balustraded balcony and parapet, and some graceful ironwork enclosing the window-sills on the ground floor. The front door was approached by a flight of steps under an important-looking glass and iron canopy.

The door was opened by a lively, pretty, fresh-looking Jewess in her early thirties, and I told her I had come in response to her advertisement. In the hall there was an air of bareness and improvisation, and there was no carpet on the stairs. She explained that she had not been long in the house and was still getting it ready, but she showed herself anxious to meet my wishes. She made some passing allusion to her husband, but he did not appear. I took a large unfurnished front room on the first floor with a bathroom adjoining it and a view of a roseate Swedenborgian church. I soon furnished it with a bed, a desk, and other necessary things, arranged for breakfasts and other meals if I wanted them, and moved in.

Beryl Fernandez, to give her a false name, was inclined to take me into her confidence, and from what she and others told me I began to form some idea of her situation. With some help from a woman friend she had the running of the house. It was not clear how her husband spent his time. I never had more than a fleeting glimpse of him and seldom even that. He was more than twenty years older than she was, and they had a little girl of six years old. There was something enigmatic and furtive about him. He was rumoured to have Mexican or American Indian blood, and it was certain that he was passionately fond of his child. I soon came to understand that Mrs Fernandez was as terrified of her husband as she was infatuated with him. His violence and threats had led her to fear that he might suddenly do her a mortal injury. This fear was shared by her woman friend. But she would not leave him or seek the protection of the law because, she said, she 'couldn't'. In fact they were madly in love with one another. The trouble was that he had fallen victim to a jealous suspicion of all other men who might even set eyes on his wife, let alone speak to her—particularly those within a radius of several miles, of course including myself. The greater their propinquity, the greater his agitation. He had nursed this suspicion until it had become a dangerous and growing delusion, and one night in November he butchered his wife in the presence of their child. I have good authority for saying that he would have butchered me in my sleep if I had not happened to be away for the weekend.

The poor, deluded woman was dead. The poor, deluded man attempted to do away with himself, but was prevented. I did not attend his trial at the Old Bailey two months later. Mr. Justice Avory, whose appearance and reputation were far from attractive, was presiding. Although a prison officer gave evidence that the accused man was suffering from delusional insanity, Fernandez was sentenced to death. An appeal was dismissed, but the death sentence was commuted to penal servitude for life. It had come out at the trial that he was an American citizen and had been a vaudeville performer of some kind.

A year or two later I wrote a novel based on the circumstances of the crime. *The Case is Altered* had some success and was chosen by the Book Society, then a fairly new institution. After the book had been in circulation for some time I received a letter from a man whose name was vaguely known to me. Let me call him Zebulon Pood. He wrote from Harley Street. He said he had been reading *The Case is Altered* with keen interest. After some compliments he said the book had a special significance for him, because it was evident to him that it had been based upon the life and death of his unfortunate cousin, Mrs Fernandez. He said I had given such a sympathetic and understanding account of her character and situation that I could no doubt tell him things he did not know about her. On the other hand, as she had not only been his cousin but one of his patients, he thought it likely that he could tell me things about her that I did not know and that might interest me. He would be so pleased if I would come and see him.

This seemed to me a faintly irregular letter. I was naturally curious to know more about the woman who had been caught up in that terrible doom, a woman whom I had known, liked, and admired, and with whom I had lived—and nearly died—under the same roof. But why should the writer assume my readiness to swap reminiscences with him? And in Harley Street! I looked him up in *Who's Who*. Dr Pood had been born in a distant country, was unmarried, and had had much and varied experience in his profession. He described himself as a sexologist and an associate of specialists and organizations concerned with sexual enlightenment and reform. He was strong on gynaecology, obstetrics, and contraception. He listed many of his articles and essays. (If we all did that, *Who's Who* would no longer be portable.) He had also written books, among them a monograph about some contraceptive contraption he had invented. I made one or two inquiries about him from worldly-wise friends about town.

'What can you tell me,' I asked, 'about Zebulon Pood?'

'The most indiscreet man in London,' was the first answer I got. It was confirmed by others. The natural curiosity of a fictionist to meet a man with that reputation was damped down. I wrote Dr Pood a civil reply and was easily able to excuse myself for not going to see him, because I was about to go abroad.

Two or three years later, when some other book of mine had come out, I think *The Invaders*, Dr Pood wrote to me again. He had just read my new book, he said. Again there were compliments. He was still hoping, he said, that some day he would have the pleasure of meeting me and exchanging recollections of his cousin, Beryl Fernandez. Well, I thought, why not? And I made an appointment to go and see him.

It was on a dark November afternoon that I found myself standing on his threshold in Harley Street. The door was opened by an uncommonly large and handsome butler. I said I was to see Dr Pood. With a slight bow, the beginnings of a Mona Lisa smile, and a pregnant silence he ushered me into a waiting room. It was furnished with the usual impersonal opulence of such places, intended no doubt in this instance to have a calming effect upon the many persons who came to Dr. Pood to have their sexological uneasinesses ironed out. Back numbers of journals about eugenics were to be seen interspersed with nice fresh copies of the *Tatler*, suitable for an invalid. Almost immediately the butler ushered me out, shut me up in a coffin-like lift, and fired me off like a guided missile to one of the upper floors.

At Home

As I stepped out I was greeted with the remark, 'You're not at all as I imagined you! I thought you would be pale and gloomy, and here you are, bursting with vitality!'

The speaker was dark and had a longish, whitish, rather flabby face, with the alert expression of a trained observer who had seen a lot of life, in this instance largely below the belt. His figure was notably pear-shaped, and enclosed in the appropriate black coat and striped trousers.

The room he led me into seemed hardly likely to be a consulting room, unless he was a sorcerer as well as a sexologist. It looked more suitable for the smoking of imitation opium, to the strains of *Chu Chin Chow*, being furnished in bad Chinese made-for-export style. It looked like a setting for a melodramatic film, an English film, about some Dr Fu or Dr Wu in Limehouse or Shanghai; with moustaches drooping like rats' tails on either side of a cynical mouth, with a diabolical urbanity, nails as long and pointed as skewers, and an abducted blonde, gagged and trussed up like a chicken, squirming unheard and unseen behind the bead curtain. I looked instinctively for the bead curtain, but in vain. The other properties were there — the excessively carved furniture and screens, the joss sticks burning in a big porcelain vase before an image of Buddha, and the bronze sconces in the form of dragons, from the mouths of which dangled the dried and spiky skins of globefish, enclosing electric light bulbs. But Dr Pood was no Fu.

'Do sit down. Ah, here's tea,' he said, as a tray was brought in by the big, reticent butler. 'Do you mind helping yourself? I never have tea myself: I prefer ginger beer. I'm very glad you've come to see me at last.' And as I poured myself out some tea he actually filled a glass with (of all things, on a black November afternoon) ginger beer.

Mrs Fernandez and Dr Pood

'You realize, of course, that my cousin's husband was suffering from general paralysis of the insane?'

I said I had supposed it might be something like that.

'And that she was passionately in love with him? She used to come and borrow money from me. She started that place, you know, on nothing. . . . He was useless, useless to her. By sticking to him she threw her life away.'

The cold suds of ginger beer made him eloquent. Her private life, her husband's sexual habits, the very questions she had put to Dr Pood about them, were now communicated to me. A man of more principle than myself would perhaps have said, 'But why are you telling me all this? It was told to you in confidence. These ought surely to be consulting room secrets. Isn't this a breach of professional etiquette as well as of personal loyalty?' What seemed to me more important was that we had something in common — that we had both liked Beryl Fernandez, had both been, in different degrees, in her confidence, and had both wished to help her. Dr. Pood *had* helped her, with professional advice, with money, and with sensible worldly advice, as her kinsman. From what I had learnt of him I knew that he was something much more than indiscreet. He was a man, so far as I could judge, entirely without puritanical prejudices, a man of great experience, with great knowledge of what used to be called human frailties — or, to be more precise, the dreadful physical and psychological muddles, fears, frustrations, and pains into which men and women are dragged by the sexual instinct. His hard-working life was devoted to easing or preventing these things. I saw him as a benevolent and beneficent man. It seemed to me that his specialized view of human life and human nature was uncommonly clear and direct. And he was amused, yes, amused, by human folly, by the grotesqueness of thought and behaviour into which we are led by the sexual impulse. Whether my doctor-like appearance made him more candid than usual I do not know, but he talked to me as if I was his equal in knowledge and understanding of gynaecology and the whole bag of tricks. Indiscreet undoubtedly, but without discernible malice.

From the subject of Beryl Fernandez and her life with her husband, we passed to a wider examination of life in London—the aspects of life to which Dr Pood's attention was drawn by his patients. He began to tell me of some divagations of the sexual instinct that had come to his notice. He was amused by some of them—and justifiably. Unless a doctor has got beyond being shocked, angered, or disgusted by what he sees and hears, he must surely be wanting in professional poise. If he has the capacity to be amused and saddened at the same time, he is likely to be a healer. Perhaps the same is true of a priest. And how the human race needs healing, inside and out!

I recall a story of Dr Pood's about a youngish man who came to consult him and admitted to a perversion that surprised even Dr Pood a little, and would to most people have seemed grotesquely unappetizing.

'Yes, I see—of course, of course,' Dr Pood said blandly, as if it were the most ordinary proceeding. 'But don't you find it rather difficult to find anybody who is willing to join you in that?'

'Oh, very difficult,' was the answer. 'And when I *do* find anybody, of course they're *never* my type!'

It requires imagination as well as tolerance to arrive at anything like a sympathetic understanding of strong emotions aroused in others by agencies that cannot even faintly begin to arouse them, or can only arouse their opposites, in oneself. Dr Pood did not seem to me an imaginative man. It was in the physiological aspects of his case-histories that he showed his understanding best, and he had that intuitive appreciation of character which is often a Jewish trait. One ludicrous yet pathetic story he told me had to do with a man well known to the public and professionally eminent. Dr Pood did not tell me the man's name, but from a fortuitous detail he let slip I was instantly able to identify him. Dr Pood might have foreseen that if I should take it into my head to go to the patient and tell what I had heard and from whom I had heard it, tremendous mischief could result, with serious consequences to this indiscreet consultant. But Dr Pood's mind evidently did not work like that. His indiscretion and trustfulness were, so to speak, part of his method as well as of his character. He did not hear the music of humanity in muffled tones; he did not see life, and did not expect his patients to see it, in a dim religious light. He seemed to treat them as fellow actors in an outrageous comedy. His directness and candour helped to make him not at all a bad specimen of a twentieth-century man—scientific; seemingly untroubled by racial or social or some important professional conventions; functioning independently and well in advance both of public opinion and of the average in his own profession; unspiritual, materialistic; inclined to make much active propaganda for what he believed helpful; and in working to save or improve human life and capabilities obviously opposed to those destructive—or, rather, self-destructive—tendencies in mankind which in this century have caused such complex and widespread suffering.

3

Evenings in Tavistock Square, Afternoons in Gower Street

WHEN I got back to my 'chambers' after that fatal weekend the woman friend of Mrs Fernandez was bearing up against distress and shock. Upon her had devolved for the time being the need to maintain the house. One of her most immediate worries was that the conjugal bedroom had not yet been put to rights. Since the police had seen it she had kept it locked. To save her a painful task I undertook to put it in order myself. She gave me the key, and with the help of the young houseman I set about removing the traces of the crime. They were copious.

Those of my friends who knew something of what had happened took it for granted that I should at once be leaving the house, and offered to put me up. I saw no reason for hurrying away. The harm had been done, and I was no longer in danger. Besides, I had sent out invitations to a small evening party and was disinclined to put off my guests.

When I had left England more than ten years before I had been too young to form any very close or settled or habitual friendships, and I had had no settled home in England. Although a repatriated person I lacked threads to take up. I had no circle to re-enter. This was not surprising; and in view of my tastes and inclinations I did not try and base my social life upon relations and connections but was drawn more to the new acquaintances my writing had made for me. Among the guests at the party was a representative of my previous life in England, Gyles Isham, with whom I had been at school. In Rugby days we used to bicycle about looking at churches. At Oxford, in the interim, he had distinguished himself as an actor, and he was to appear later with Greta Garbo in *Anna Karenina*. He brought his sister, Virginia; I wanted them to meet Virginia Woolf, to whom they were related. South Africa was represented by Edward Wolfe, the painter, and his mother. Virginia Woolf came with her husband, Leonard Woolf. I had also invited Anthony Butts and his mother, Mary Colville-Hyde. We assembled in a somewhat cavernous room with moss-green walls and one of those massive Bayswater chimneypieces made of great slabs of Italian marble. This was Victorian London all right; Frith had had his studio only a few doors away; and near at hand was Westbourne Grove, where some of the contents of the shops, and some of the shoppers, could have altered little since the nineties. With her acute sensitiveness to atmosphere Virginia Woolf looked about her with interest; with her intense curiosity about human beings she engaged her fellow guests in conversation.

I was now just twenty-six, and several years had passed since the publication in London of my first novel, the manuscript of which had travelled some six thousand miles to the Hogarth Press. I had also published two books of short stories. Like the novel they had been well received — at least in some quarters — and I had therefore in some respects more self-confidence than I should have had if I had not yet published anything. To have known from the first that Leonard and Virginia Woolf believed in me as a writer had been much; to have been published by them was more still. The welcome they gave me when I returned to England, and their subsequent friendship, I value as much as anything in my life. Leonard Woolf used to send me books for review in the *Nation*, of which he was then literary editor, and soon after my return they had been good enough to invite me to the first of a long series of evenings in Tavistock Square. Besides enjoying their beautiful manners, incomparable conversation, and delicious food and wine, I was enabled to meet there for the first time many persons of literary distinction or unusual character. For a young writer, obscure, socially and by experience and temperament rather isolated, poor, curious, and both leisurely and energetic, these evenings were of such benefit and pleasure, such an education in themselves, that I strongly hope there are young writers to-day who find themselves half as delightfully and fruitfully entertained.

In the upper room to which withdrawal was made after dinner the lighting was fairly subdued, otherwise attention might have been unduly distracted by the mural decorations from the hand of Virginia Woolf's sister, Mrs Bell. In fact these rough trellises and wavy lines, two-handled vases, guitars, fans, and sketchy floral motifs, made their contribution to the unsolemn atmosphere of a room not quite like any other. Virginia Woolf, equally adept at entertaining and being entertained, unobtrusively kept those present as active, or attentive, as an orchestra, and unless some visitor was awkward, shy, or moody, the tempo was lively and the tone gay.

A card would have reached me, and her handwriting, sharp, delicate, and rhythmical as her prose, was pleasing in itself—the more so because it had formed an invitation; and there was often added, as if by way of an afterthought, 'X. is coming.' X. was almost always somebody eminent in the sphere of writing. Only a week or two after the murder a card of invitation had reached me. 'Lytton Strachey is coming,' it said.

Evenings in Tavistock Square

Strachey was then still in his forties, but his beard and spectacles made him look older. Although he was lanky and Edward Lear was rotund, I imagine that Lear's beard and spectacles may also have seemed to create a certain distance between himself and others. About Strachey's eyelids, as he looked out through the windows of his spectacles over the quickset hedge of his beard, there was a suggestion of world-weariness: he had in fact just two more years to live. To me he did not seem like a man in early middle age, and although his beard made him look older than he was, I did not think of him in terms of a sum of years but as an intelligence alert and busy behind the appendage of hair and the glass outworks. A glint came into his eyes, the brain was on the move as swiftly as a bat, with something of the radar-like sensitivity of a bat, and when he spoke it was sometimes in the voice of a bat.

There was a story that in the first World War he had been summoned before some military tribunal, and had appeared before it tall, sad, spectacled, bearded, and carrying a tartan travelling rug and an air cushion. Applying the air cushion to the aperture in his beard he had slowly and gravely inflated it, had then put it on the seat, subsided gently upon it, and carefully and deliberately arranged the rug over his knees. A brisk military voice had then fired at him from the bench:

'We understand, Mr. Strachey, that you are against *all* wars?'

'No,' came the piercing little voice of the pipistrel from the thicket. 'Only this one.'

I am glad to have set eyes upon this wit and revolutionary biographer, a master of English prose, so entertaining and such an influence. It happened that much later in my own life I was to have a particular reason for pondering over the workings of Strachey's mind in regard to certain historical characters.

At Home

Benjamin Britten's opera *Gloriana*, which was produced at the time of Queen Elizabeth II's coronation, and for which I wrote the libretto, owed much to Strachey's *Elizabeth and Essex*.

Quite a different voice from Strachey's came crackling, dry and vibrant and precise, out of the intellectual head of Roger Fry, whose spectacles seemed to magnify both ways. To look him in the eyes was to look through twin lenses at two keen and magnified visual organs and simultaneously to be conscious of exposure to expert scrutiny. If one had been anywhere overpainted, or badly varnished, or if one had been wearing the exasperating label of a false attribution, one could hardly have gone on looking him in the face. His devotion to 'significant form' is pleasantly illustrated by the story that he was seen in the National Gallery lecturing about the composition of a large religious masterpiece to a docile squad of gaping self-improvers. Indicating with his long wooden pointer the presiding figure of God the Father, he was heard to say, 'Now, this important mass . . .'

Fry's own pictures have generally seemed to me saddish confections, like those of an amateur cook with sound training and well tried recipes but without the least spark of inspiration. He had been engaged by the Hogarth Press to design the dust jacket for my book of short stories on Japanese themes, *Paper Houses*. Though not at all Japanese in feeling, it was a pleasing design in blue and white, and aroused regret that dust jackets are such perishable things.

It was at Tavistock Square that I first met Lady Ottoline Morrell, who, once seen, could not be forgotten. About so legendary a figure there must surely be sooner or later much to be collected and made known: she is believed to have been far from neglect by writers of fiction. Her bearing was impressive. As was not unusual with women of her generation and of orderly upbringing, she held herself so straight-backed that she gave an impression of being taller than she was. There was style and dignity in her movements, even if the style of her clothes and ornaments was sometimes that of fancy dress. The first time I saw her she was wearing in her frizzed-out, reddish hair several quoit-like rings of what looked like reddish amber, and very full and stiff and sibilant shot-silk shirts, which set up a tremendous whispering campaign every time she moved. Her large-boned head, held rather high, with its commanding nose and chin, and her long, bony fingers helped to give her an air of authority. Her voice, nasal but not unpleasant, and with a curious and indescribable timbre, confidential and almost conspiratorial, caught and held one's attention.

If she had a streak of unwisdom, if her interest in writers and painters and in their personal affairs was held to be sometimes intrusive or even scheming, that did not trouble me. I was purposely not very responsive to direct inquiries about my private life, and when a young poet (now famous) asked her what she thought of me she said (according to his account):

'A very nice man—but he's just like a pump! I *pump* and *pump*, and I *can't* get anything out of him!'

She had, all the same, got this young poet out of me. With her flair for creative talent and promise she had taken note of his name and work at a very early stage of his career; she knew I knew him; and she had urged me to introduce him to her at one of her afternoons in Gower Street. I had accordingly done so, and I think those afternoons were as much of a benefit and pleasure to him as they had already been to me. They enabled us to meet W. B. Yeats and T. S. Eliot, and to hear the fluent speech of one and the carefully weighed and measured speech of the other.

At Home

'And do you often go back to America?' a friend of mine asked Eliot in my hearing at about this time.

'Not very often.' A pause, while he looked at the floor with great concentration: his answer must not offend any of his principles, nor militate against truth, logic, or the established religion. 'On an average,' he said, and then again paused, perhaps to consider the possible ramifications of the effect of what he was about to say, 'I should say about every twenty years.'

Less celebrated poets were to be seen in attendance at Gower Street—a contemporary of Yeats's, for instance, whose unexcited demeanour and no doubt harmless writings had earned him the nickname 'The Sheep in Sheep's Clothing'. It was said that in one of his poems the two following lines occurred:

> She was as old as any rose,
> And older than most sheep.

I cannot vouch for the truth of this, but the lines do not seem out of character. At Gower Street, too, could be seen a gnome-like Irish writer, James Stephens. Seated in a corner, Stephens was heard by me to say one afternoon, in a thickish brogue, apparently without irony, and intending to clinch an argument, 'After all, the Little People always know best.' This piece of Celtic twaddle was too much for the strict Cambridge rationalism of Leonard Woolf, who happened to be present and to have been listening to Stephens with mounting exasperation, and now said testily, and with unconcealed disgust, 'Nonsense! *Nonsense!*'

These afternoons in Gower Street, with their celebrities and often good conversation, could I suppose be described as a salon. They were valuable for a young writer. I am not ashamed of having been pleased by the interest Lady Ottoline expressed in my writings. When T. S. Eliot lent her my novel *Sado* she took the trouble to write and tell me what she thought about it, and when I sent her *The Case is Altered* she wrote to me at length with an appreciation of character and incident that seemed as genuine as it was detailed. Her letters, written in brown ink, a rococo script unlike anything else on earth, and in a style which seemed to owe something to Mr Jingle and something to Ronald Firbank, have been hilariously described by Stephen Spender in *World Within World*. I had in those days some aptitude for graphological analysis, which later went into abeyance, and even if I had never seen her or known her I should have found them revealing of a character both original and impressive.

She was, I suppose, the only person I am likely to have known who began life with the 'double blessing' (as her half brother, the Duke of Portland, put it) of being kissed both by the Prince of Wales (later Edward VII) and Disraeli. I always think of this when passing Disraeli's house in Curzon Street, and also of my father as a boy being sent across every morning after breakfast from my grandfather's house in Chesterfield Street to read the bulletins outside the house when the great man lay dying. I like these links and fortuitous associations with the past. They lend perspective to the great turmoil of life.

Of Lady Ottoline it may be said, in a phrase much hackneyed by amateur obituarists, that we shall not look upon her like again — but then, who had ever looked upon it before? That she was not a type but an individual was the primary thing that her handwriting proclaimed. Style, warmth, enterprise, and a passionate respect for creativeness in the arts were among her attributes. She was easy game, or rich material, for satirists. She is said to have been a mainstay, a breadwinner almost, for certain satirical novelists of the twenties who had made use of her hospitality and friendship. Something of an anthology could be made of fictional characters in prose—and in verse too—who might be supposed to be gay traducements of this uncommon woman. Perhaps not enough has been made of the courage she showed in being a rebel. Without knowing it, she occasioned one of the most old world or feudal remarks I have ever heard. Far from London an old noblewoman, hearing Lady Ottoline praised as a patron of the arts, said with some severity, 'But she has betrayed our Order.'* I remember Virginia Woolf's astonishment when I repeated this anachronism to her.

Once when Virginia Woolf was sitting beside Lady Ottoline on a sofa their two profiles were suddenly to be seen, one in relief against the other, like two profiles on some Renaissance medal—two strange, queenly figures evolved in the leisured and ceremonious days of the nineteenth century. Each, by being herself, won an allegiance to herself in the twentieth. Both faces were aristocratic, but in that chance propinquity Virginia Woolf's appeared much the more fine and delicate. The two women admired one another, with reservations on one side at least; and they were affectionate in manner when together, though one appeared more affectionate than the other. They had a good deal in common. Both had what old-fashioned people used to call *presence*—a kind of stateliness, a kind of simple, unfussy dignity. Lady Ottoline Morrell, not always discriminating about people, recognized the uniqueness of Virginia Woolf. Virginia Woolf spoke admiringly of the independence and force of character

---

* The other remark has nothing to do with Lady Ottoline, but seems worth preserving in a footnote. A prince (half Prussian) of a reigning royal house, having to move out of a small private room into a large room where it was his and his wife's duty to mingle and talk with an expectant crowd of dressed up citizenry, glanced at a clock, took her by the hand, and said, 'Come along, X., it's time *to charge the mob.*'

which had enabled Lady Ottoline to emerge from the grand but narrow world into which she had been born (and of which she retained the panache) into a more varied world in which ideas and talent counted more than property or background.

Both had an insatiable curiosity about their fellow creatures, and both a love of gossip and the capacity to be amused or astonished which goes with that virtue. In the exercise of this curiosity the difference of approach was as striking as the difference in their profiles. Lady Ottoline would ask the most personal, direct questions, not in a hectoring way, but without the slightest compunction, and with the manner of a feudal grandee who had a right to be told what she wanted to know. Because most people like talking about themselves to a sympathetc listener she often got what she wanted, but not, as I have indicated, from me. Virginia Woolf's approach was less blunt and more ingenious. With a delicious and playful inventiveness she would often improvise an ironical fantasy about the life and habits of the person to whom she was talking, and this was likely to call forth protests, denials, and explanations which helped to make up something like a confession. Lady Ottoline, less tense and less discerning, was an easier mixer: Virginia Woolf sometimes frightened people by aloofness or asperity, for which they had sometimes their own clumsiness to blame. Yet she could show the most graceful restraint. In the course of several hours of the company of an individual who, she afterwards told me, caused her alternating emotions of anger, laughter, and utter boredom, she showed no sign of the first two and only a faint trace of the last — which is the most difficult of the three to hide.

The fact that Virginia Woolf did not make, either in social life or in her books, any concession to vulgarians, or offer any foothold to a banal understanding, or bait any traps for popularity, probably helped to create a legend about herself among the un-informed, the envious, and the ignorant, that she was some sort of precious and fragile being, ineffably superior and aloof, and quite out of touch with 'ordinary' life — whatever that may be. This legend has been completely dispersed. It is now understood that her life was rich in experience of people and places, and that her disposition, as is sometimes the case with those who are highly strung and have an inclination to melancholy, was genial. Her biographers, so far from having to chronicle the life of an etiolated recluse, may be embarrassed by the quantity and variety of their material. Clearly no adequate biography will be possible until her immense diary has been published in full. From her con-versation I recall many interesting glimpses and facets of her earlier life—how, as a young girl, in an agony of shyness, she drove alone at night in a cab with straw on the floor to a ball at one of the great London houses, wearing no jewellery except a modest string of pearls ('but they were *real* pearls'); how she had Greek lessons with Clara, the sister of Walter Pater, in Canning Place, in a setting of blue china, Persian cats, and Morris wallpapers; how she took part in the Dreadnought Hoax, one of the world's great practical jokes and a superb piece of acting, a demonstration that high-ranking hearts of oak at Portsmouth were accompanied by heads of the same material, since they were unable to see through a bogus Negus of Abyssinia and his pre-posterous 'suite'; how she went bathing with Rupert Brooke, whose profile was not quite lived up to by his legs, those being perceptibly bowed; how she sat up all night in a Balkan hotel reading the *Christian Science Monitor* to cheat the bugs; and how there was a murder under her window in Euboea.

Speaking of writing as a profession, she once remarked to me that one is bound to upset oneself physically if one works for more than two hours a day. She put so much of herself into her work that it must have taken much out of her, and was in fact a prodigiously hard worker. The volume of her published and unpublished writings, including her letters and diary, is as impressive as the sustained high level of all that has so far been printed. She was as energetic as her father, to whom mountains were no obstacles, nor mountains of facts either. To be so active, one's nature must be integrated. In each of us there are two beings, one solitary and one social. There are persons who cannot bear to be with others, and turn into hermits or something worse; most cannot bear to be alone, and become common or shallow, or both. In Virginia Woolf the two beings seemed to have an equal life and so to make her into a complete person. She could be detached and see things in perspective; and she could enter into things, into other people's lives, until she became part of them. The two beings can be perceived in her writings, sometimes distinct, sometimes merged. The special genius of her rare and solitary spirit reached its purest expression in *The Waves*, an exquisite, subjective book nearer to poetry and music than to what is generally meant by 'the novel'. The social being in Virginia Woolf, and (in my opinion) the novelist, can be seen most clearly not in her fiction but in *The Common Reader*. Those essays are full of shrewdness and knowledge of the world and of human nature, qualities which, though discernible in her novels, are less important to them than her own sensitivity, as an instrument to the vibrations of the external world.

The old masters of fiction—Shakespeare, Balzac, Tolstoy—are such because, besides all the other gifts, they are imaginative men of the world with an exceptional robustness and gusto. They have also an extreme preoccupation with sociology. This, when it goes more with finesse than with animal spirits, produces

At Home

novelists like Jane Austen, Flaubert, or Proust, and it was to such writers that Virginia Woolf was in some ways akin. It may be argued that her myth-making faculty was chiefly applied to sensations rather than to characters, and that her passion for sociology was in a sense scientific. Although she enjoyed embroidering facts about people, sometimes in a poetic or a fantastic or a censorious or an ironical way, she was really devoted to the facts themselves. The solitary being was a poet, the social being was a sort of scientist: the former discovered poetic truth, the latter anthropological truth.

During the last ten years of her life Virginia Woolf often told me how much more she enjoyed reading autobiographies than novels. She once said that she thought almost any autobiography more satisfying than a novel. When autobiographical memoirs were written by people she knew and found congenial—Lady Oxford, for instance (and what a sharp profile there!) or the bluff and breezy Dame Ethel Smyth—she not only had the pleasure of getting to know them better, but her appetite for social knowledge and reminiscence was much gratified. A passionate precision in collecting data about society (very strong in Flaubert and Proust) made her delight in anything that helped it.

At those evenings in Tavistock Square she was at her best with persons who, like herself, were not merely articulate but articulate in a new way. She had a gift for making the young and obscure feel that they were of value too. She admired physical as well as intellectual beauty. She could charm away diffidence, and, since she was something of a feminist, could be notably sympathetic with young women, in particular young women from Cambridge. A strong sense of the proper functions of literature and a highly and constantly cultivated taste gave her a proper pride (derived in part no doubt from her literary father and background) in her own gifts, but she was without arrogance, and wore her rare beauty without ostentation.

It is not enough to say that she was a hard-working writer, and that she always read a great deal. She also worked as a publisher, and even at times as a printer, with her husband. She examined a great number of typescripts and even of manuscripts for the Hogarth Press, books from which rightly bore the imprint of 'Leonard and Virginia Woolf'. No writer, known or unknown, could have wished for a more encouraging publisher's reader, or one with more openness to new ideas. She seemed unimpeded by prejudice and guided always by the knowledge that the true writer is a precision instrument with something unfamiliar to record. As early as 1930 she and her husband expressed some annoyance at the way the Hogarth Press was developing. They even seemed rather annoyed by the increasingly profitable sales of Hogarth Press books, and were seriously considering reducing the press to its original and remarkable dimensions — a hand press in a basement at Richmond, worked by themselves as amateurs. This was before John Lehmann was inducted into the business and began his long and conspicuous career as a publisher and editor. From the time I first saw him he showed an interest in my writings which has continued to this day, and I am only one of innumerable writers whom he has helped.

The nervous vitality of Virginia Woolf was greater than her physical strength. If it had not been so, she would not have gone on evoking such a response from the responsive in so many parts of the world. To write about her briefly is to be inadequate. She was complex. She looked for truth. She loved London and the country, her relations and friends; she loved her domestic surroundings; she loved the written word. She liked good talk, good food, and good coffee. I see her in a shady hat and summer sleeves, moving between the fig tree and the zinnias at Rodmell; I see her sitting over a fire and smoking one of her favourite cheroots; I see the nervous shoulders, the thin, creative wrists, the unprecedented sculpture of the temples and eye sockets. I see her grave and introspective, or in such a paroxysm of laughter that the tears came into her eyes. But her eyes are shut, and I shall never see her again.

4

Grand Chain

IHAVE said that I lacked a circle to re-enter, but the word 'circle' is distasteful, with its suggestion of clique or coterie, and I have an innate disinclination for hunting in a pack. Not everybody I met at Tavistock Square was new to me. I remember Virginia Woolf being surprised, when she introduced me to the beautiful Rosamond Lehmann, that I knew her already. A straight and slender neck supported a head carried with an adventurous tilt. The hair springing from the finely modelled forehead, the high colour on the salient cheekbones, and the eyes with their prevalent expression of attentive amazement seemed an embodiment of eagerness and expectancy. But sometimes the mouth lost its playful tenderness and looked sad and resigned, and the eyes were fixed in a blank, faraway look. Her brother and sisters are all physically impressive and unlike one another. Perhaps they owe their unusualness to their mixed ancestry, of which John Lehmann has spoken in *The Whispering Gallery*. I never saw their father, but their mother, even in old age, was uncommonly handsome. Of John Lehmann's light-blue eyes, sometimes disconcertingly narrowed in moments of scepticism, inquiry, or disapproval, and set in a head without fleshy padding, someone had said, 'Those eyes! Like forget-me-nots inside a skull!' His svelte sister Helen has so deep a voice that it never ceases to be a delightful surprise every time she speaks. And his sister Beatrix, whose vibrant performance in *Mourning Becomes Electra* almost made

57

one forget the poverty of its author's language, has a face upon which the masks of tragedy and comedy succeed one another so rapidly that they become one, just as the wings of a hover-fly vibrate so quickly that they almost, but never quite, appear static.

Virginia Woolf's discovery that I already knew Rosamond Lehmann aroused her highly characteristic professional curiosity. She was agog to know *how*, *when*, and *where*. Writers of memoirs often say nothing about the most usual process by which acquaintance is extended. It is like the movement in the Lancers which used to be enjoyed by children of my generation at their dancing classes and was known as 'the Grand Chain'. I first met Rosamond Lehmann with Stephen Spender, then still an undergraduate at Oxford. His home was in Frognal, at Hampstead, an establishment he has described in his autobiography. Directed by remote control by a rather formidable grandmother—a troglodyte in the comfortable gloom of a mansion flat near the Albert Hall—it was managed by a pair of devoted but perhaps rather strict family servants who had developed a composite personality. These two excellent women had therefore been given a composite name and, to an occasional visitor, had an inseparable identity. They maintained at Frognal a clinical cleanliness, and exercised a sort of jaunty strictness over the orphaned Spenders. The eldest brother seemed to be away a good deal; the quiet Humphrey and the sister, Christine, with her enigmatic smile, listened in fascinated and affectionate silence to the gay and spontaneous talk of their brother Stephen, in which acuteness mingled with a certain naivety, innocence with sophistication, unworldliness with ambition, benevolence with a strain of satire. No wonder their attention was held: here was a young poet 'bursting' (to repeat Dr. Pood's phrase) 'with vitality' and aimed at the future like a rocket. The freshness, candour, and newness of his early poems has re-emerged in later ones. It is one of the advantages of middle age to have been able to watch the development of the characters and talents of one's friends. Sometimes success and maturity fit them out in the hard, crustacean shell of the impatient public man, so that their early tenderness becomes little more than a memory. Sometimes bitterness of experience, or the influence of a wife or mistress, changes their nature or inflates their self-importance. Sometimes they deteriorate, through loneliness, or drink, or vagabond desires, or illness, or disappointment. But none of these things has happened to Stephen Spender. Happy in his wife and children, he pursues his course without a sign of diminished energy or gaiety.

I had first met him in Egerton Terrace, at the flat of René Janin, who was the son of a French general and who had what may be called social curiosity. He was able to exercise this even when young with what seemed an innate knowledge of the world but was in fact an aplomb seldom to be seen in an Englishman of his age. With his good looks, his intelligence and ability, he might understandably have been a little vain, but he seemed without illusions: any melancholy that may have resulted (as it may from such a cause) was made almost imperceptible by his rare capacity to amuse and to be amused. He seemed to have a fixed standard of traditional beliefs in political matters. Compared with, let us say, Stephen Spender he seemed a reactionary surviving from some *ancien régime*, but that put him in the strong position of mistrusting the loud-voiced demagogues, villains, and madmen of our time who were trusted by millions and ruined Europe. He moved and still moves with equal ease and amusement in social, intellectual, diplomatic, and commercial spheres in any country where English, French, German, or Spanish are spoken, and like most of his contemporaries he has needed fortitude to bring him through to the present day.

René Janin I had first seen in the company of Laurens van der Post, with whom I had left Africa for Japan, as I have described in an earlier book. Laurens van der Post was now married and a father, and had settled in London—if settled is the word for one who had a long way to go before he found full scope for his energies. In the early Thirties he wrote a novel about South Africa, for which I had the pleasure of finding a title in the Bible. *In a Province* is a book with a place of some significance in the interesting evolution of the South African novel, but in those days it attracted less attention than many less valuable books later, when South Africa had again become more topical. Then his natural inclination to the open air and his liking for animals took him, a few years later, off to the Cotswolds, where he acquired a farm and where I used to visit him.

Sometimes I encountered persons with whom I had made contact by post. When still very young I had sent some poems to Harold Monro, who had written encouragingly to me in Africa. And now, in a mixed gathering one evening in London, 'There's Harold Monro,' said one of his contemporaries, and then called out to him in a mocking voice, 'Monro! Miaow, *miaow!*'

Monro turned, looked displeased, and said in a serious tone: 'That's a *good* poem, Z. That's a *good* poem.'

The allusion was to a poem of Monro's called 'Milk for the Cat', which in those days was widely familiar and had earned him, so he told people, a then surprising sum of money in anthology fees.

I looked at Monro with respectful curiosity, and was introduced to him. His poetry is by no means all so gently domesticated and descriptive as the poem about the cat: it used to seem to me like the voice of someone somehow encaged or immured and trying in vain to get out. As a boy at Rugby I had bought 'rhyme sheets' from the Poetry Bookshop to hang on my wall, best of all Walter de la Mare's 'Arabia' with gaudy decorations by Lovat Fraser: I soon knew it by heart. The successive volumes of *Georgian Poetry*, breaking in upon the post-Victorian twilight, had been quickening to many readers of my generation. I had lately visited the Poetry Bookshop for the first time, with its temple-like atmosphere and its polychromatic lining of 'slim volumes'; but it seemed already to belong to the past. Guerrilla warfare had already broken out in the earliest printed poems of W. H. Auden.

It would be untrue to say that I was wholly engaged in dancing the Grand Chain. I was often alone. For some writers it may be enjoyable to be steeped in alcohol, it may be necessary: but not for me, who had other weaknesses. I was in any case shy, and had not yet adjusted myself to English life. For some writers, when young at least, it is habitual to go into a huddle for twenty-four hours out of every twenty-four with half-baked devotees of the arts, persons of both sexes often with no visible means of subsistence or fixed abode (who make up the fringe, pretty frayed in places, of the serious world inhabited by serious artists), in pubs, clubs, studios, and beds. Again, not for me. I was more inclined to haunt picture galleries, old and new. I have a visual, or pictorial, imagination, and it needed training by looking at all sorts of pictures very often. In Africa I had been deprived of this exercise, in the Far East I had accustomed my eyes to Chinese paintings and the decorative arts of Japan. Much as they had helped me, they had not been enough. I had craved for the arts of Europe, and now I pursued my visual education with lusting eyes. Of all European painters the two who stirred me most at this time hardly made a pair — Millet and Poussin. In London and Paris I pursued them both. In Millet a kind of earthy goodness, wholly West-European, and in Poussin the classical myths, the rigid, immortal gestures, and the yellow draperies in an eternal-seeming golden light combined to appease some appetite in me; they took away the feeling of impoverishment, of aesthetic displacement. And for a stimulant there were the newest Picassos.

Is there such a word as re-occidentation? The process it denotes was not altogether easy for me, the process of readapting myself to life in England. In many ways it seemed to me an alien country, in some ways it does still, in certain beliefs, habits, pleasures. What irregular features and physiques the English had! How dirty most of them were! How peculiar they smelt in public places! Why were they often cruel to children? Why did they in any case bring them up so badly, too strictly or too neglectfully? Why were they cynomaniacs? And why, being so, did they treat their dogs with such a lack of understanding? Why had they made a cult of cricket? There was no end to my questions. Daily life was strange enough. How clumsy to eat with a great metal implement in each hand instead of with chopsticks in one! And how strange not to sleep on the floor, but nightly to be extended, Mazeppa-like, on the back of an inanimate quadruped with a tendency to squeak or creak!

Perhaps what shocked me most was the theatre. It was not that I was an addict, but I was less of one when confronted with imbecile plays of what might be called an unreal realism. The curtain went up on a room with a door at each end and always a french window at the back, and the entrances and exits were so obvious that one could generally foresee them. Use was made of a telephone on a table, and there was nearly always a servant, who was represented as comic — too dignified or too vulgar or too uneducated. No wonder domestic service, which is an honourable calling, became despised. It would have been intolerable to work for these men with falsely hearty and women with falsely genteel voices. Evidently strangers to acting, they spoke lifeless words strung together by some uninventive hack and leavened with cheap or puerile witticisms. One's attention was dragged through some anaemic succession of stale contrivings and blatant insignificance, and, if one happened to be the guest of somebody one did not know very well, the effort of keeping the jaws clamped against the giant yawns continually trying to escape almost led to lockjaw.

I was not used to this sort of thing. I was used to the tension, the visual splendour, the stylized diction and posture, and the schooled, hereditary actors of the Kabuki. I was used to professional acting that could make an old man in the part of a young girl more like a young girl than any young girl could possibly be. These English offerings had not the remotest connection of any kind with the even more stylized, the noble and hieratic No plays, where an actor standing masked and motionless in a formalized envelope of stiff sumptuous brocade seemed on a supra-human level, until, to a palpitation of drumbeats, he slowly, slowly raised one waxen hand, with the fingers joined, and held it in front of his face to signify grief, and one's whole being was agitated and torn by the extreme pathos of the moment and the movement, which brought out the inmost humanity of this unrealistic figure and joined it, as if electrically, to the inmost humanity of the audience. No wonder, I thought, that the Japanese regarded Europeans as barbarians and went for them (barbarously) with two-handed swords.

As for the snobbish, would-be satirical plays of the period, and the wet, sickly, sub-romantic musical fantasies, they seemed decadence itself. And I remember no critic then who had, for instance, the directness, sharpness, and verbal dexterity of Kenneth Tynan in dealing with them. But in the music halls and cabarets there were to be found studied, finished, original performances perfect in their way—Nellie Wallace with her insecure aigrette and trapped in her too tight silver lamé evening dress, or Douglas Byng with his grotesque impersonations and improprieties:

> In two yards of tulle I could break every rule
> And still keep the censor at bay,

or

> A bit hard to go wrong on a marble chaise-longue,
> But never too hard for me.

Perhaps in a moment of irritation—and not only irritation but exasperation must at times be allowed to exiles—an Englishman in Japan had said to me, 'The Japanese will never be civilized until they have a Mozart and a Middlesex Hospital.' All he really meant, I suppose, was that he himself had a longing for the best of the West, in whatever form. That same longing had brought me back to Europe, to England, to London, and how wonderful were the achievements with which, in fact, I was surrounded! Gyles Isham took me to see Gielgud in *Richard II*, and although it was too evidently a one-man show, the play seemed made for the actor, the actor for the play. With a temperament, a technique, and a sense of the sublime language he had to use, he played his part as a musician of the first class plays a first class instrument. And when I took my mother to hear Edith Sitwell reading her own poems to a small public audience, all was well again. A rare nature with rare bones; a face and hands that might have belonged to a daughter of one of those "Angevin dim Kings"; a manner without the least taint of affectation or pomposity. There was a dignity that seemed as if it might sharpen into asperity; an underlying compassion in the voice and in the shape of the eyelids; an easily accessible sense of the ridiculous, the impertinent, and the commonplace. The poetry of Edith Sitwell was not new to me. It must have been about 1920 that I had sent to England from Johannesburg for *The Wooden Pegasus*, and when the book arrived, in its bright magenta cover, it confirmed that she had obeyed the summons of the ninety-eighth Psalm, a summons which only a poet is able to obey:

> O sing unto the Lord a new song: for he hath done
> marvellous things.

Not long after this I heard her reading with her two brothers at a full dress evening gathering in a private house in Mayfair. This time there seemed a slight lack of rapport with the audience, as if performers and hearers did not quite trust one another. There did not seem any reason why they should, nor was it possible to imagine a bridging of the gulf between them. The three profiles made a memorable ensemble. A commando troop, the Sitwells had originated and led a resistance movement against the philistinism of their own class. The distinction of their own writings is inseparable from their devotion to the fine arts, and it is not often enough remembered how much they have done to help, to appreciate, and to draw attention to the works of writers younger than themselves. It was not until later that I came to know them personally, but I had been the more gratified at an early stage by Osbert Sitwell's interest in my writings because I already admired his own. As a wit, a satirist, a writer of fiction, and an autobiographer, he has maintained an independence that can best be called aristocratic. During the Second World War, when a good many people suddenly took to reading Trollope, my preferred authors were Gibbon, Balzac, Gissing, Firbank, and Osbert Sitwell.

I have been lucky in the friends I have made through my writings, and there was one who played a special part in my re-adaptation to Western life. While living in Japan I had received a fan letter from an Englishman whose name was new to me. He wrote from Taormina. It was an effusive letter, full of adjectives. The writer evidently did not see life—or literature—in half-tones. He kept using words like extreme, profound, deep, amazing, blinding, extraordinary, sheer, exquisite, dynamic, icy, terrible, immense, superb, vast, penetrating, hideous. I hasten to say that they were not all applied to me and my fictions. But if he lacked moderation, most people, after all, lack anything else. And he had understood what I was driving at in my earliest published writings, and had on the whole approved of the way I drove. What had most interested him was what he called my analysis of the impact of the European upon the African. He had seen, he said, something of the effect of Western materialism in Asia, and he thought it was beginning to make life unliveable even in Europe and had failed to evolve any belief by which men could live in the future. He felt that the African could only try and maintain his identity by taking over the white man's techniques, and yet that in doing so he would in fact cease to be himself. He thought Africa ought, all the same, to revert to the African. His name was Anthony Butts.

There are a good many people living who knew him, but I doubt if anybody knew him as well as I did. I wrote and told him of my return to England, and a close friendship began which lasted to his death. In many ways he was unusual. A descendant of Sir William Butts, who is a character in Shakespeare's *King Henry the Eighth*, he came of a family of Norfolk origin. His great-grandfather was Thomas Butts, the friend and patron of Blake. He himself was born in 1900, the son of an old man with a young wife. His own father had in fact been born in 1830, and his grandfather could remember having been held up as a child in the arms of a nurse who showed him the portrait of a lady and said, 'That is the poor Queen of France, whose head was cut off the day before yesterday.' So Anthony Butts, almost my coeval, was rooted in the already remote past. I suppose that being an old man's son must have affected his physique, appearance, and disposition. His premature baldness, large luminous eyes, and at times eccentric behaviour or conversation caused persons who did not like him to think him a booby or zany. I did not find him that, but his character was admittedly somewhat extravagant.

After his father's death his mother had married again. He had not liked his stepfather, Freddy Colville-Hyde, and his early experiences of family life had made him cynical. A complication was that he had an elder sister, Mary, who hated her mother and was neither liked not trusted by Anthony himself. She wrote books. They had a tone of precious knowingness, and the fatal limitation of being too much of their period. In a sense they were vulgar: J. B. Yeats, writing of the paintings of Orpen, defined vulgarity as 'the excess of the means of the expression over the content'. I do not mean to imply that the writings of Mary Butts had anything like the technical brilliance of Orpen's paintings, but they did show excess of manner over matter. They had for a time a certain vogue. She also wrote an autobiography, about which the most memorable thing was not modesty, nor good sense, nor veracity, but the frontispiece—a reproduction of a drawing of the author by Cocteau.

As a very young man, her brother found himself rich, lively, and without responsibilities or clearly defined ambitions, or any one strong bent. He was fond of pleasure and travel, and had some knowledge of music and literature and much of painting, for which he had marked talent. He was sociable and a brilliant raconteur, and it cannot be said that in his late twenties, when I first knew him, he had done much except amuse himself. But he was not merely a playboy. He was entirely serious in his intention to develop his talent for painting, and he had an instinct for what was sound in people or creative in the arts. Underneath the sometimes wild frivolity and immoderate satire of his conversation he was haunted by a sense of the tragic future. This too may have had something to do with his having been the offspring of an old man, but I believe it had much more to do with imagination and intuition. He had an acute sense that the society which had produced him was dislocated and doomed: so had many psychologically or socially maladjusted young men and women in those days, and it made some of them look to what they believed to be Communism as what they believed to be the hope of a better world. If he was maladjusted, that very fact is a criticism of his background and education; if he was early disillusioned, it was not his fault. Even before the Twenties were out he had no doubt that there would soon be another World War. It was perhaps his sense of the destructiveness, and self-destructiveness, of Western civilization which had reinforced his admiration for other races and cultures than those of Europe and North America.

It would be false to suggest that there was anything obsessive about his negrophilism, but I think it worth some further comment. Many men and women in London and elsewhere in the West during the Twenties were attracted by coloured people. Coloured singers and dancers, jazz music and dancing from America — African in remote origin and best executed by performers of African descent—had been making a strong impact, and personal acquaintance with them was for many youngish English men and women something new and exciting. To the young and frivolous such acquaintance promised new sensations and a chance to startle the staid, or to annoy their own parents; and the cultivation of coloured acquaintances, even to the point of intimacy, became a fashion. It would be a mistake to suppose that to be young and well off in the Twenties, or the Thirties either, was necessarily to be wholly frivolous or merely fashionable. When a strong sympathy with the coloured races, amounting to partisanship, showed itself in some persons of intellect and sensibility, this was put down by those who could not understand it to unbalance or a perverse sexual attraction. But it is at least possible that this sympathy may have been something more than an attraction of opposites, of white skins to black, or of nervous and complex natures to natures supposedly simple and comparatively carefree. Did it not perhaps foreshadow the collapse of what has lately come to be called colonialism, and the emergence of that entirely fresh attitude to racial differences which necessity now demands? That such a sympathy, with arguments of some weight to justify it, should have arisen in Anthony Butts, a lively young Englishman of the propertied class, schooled at Eton, and with no boyhood experience of any country but England seems to me to have much to do with the fact that he was a child of the century with something of the unconscious prescience that is found in visionaries.

Under his roof, or that of his mother, Mrs. Colville-Hyde, I was to meet a number of interesting people, but only one Negro, in the shape of Paul Robeson. He was then at the height of his vocal powers, and his imposing physical presence and candid manner seemed to be the index of largeness of outlook and a genial humanity. He was accompanied by his lively wife, who later made a tour of Africa and wrote a book about it.

When Stephen Spender asked me to Oxford to address the English Society, Anthony Butts travelled with me and we put up at the Mitre. The next day we took Julian Green, who was with us, round to see the sights of Oxford — a town to which I was no stranger, and which I remembered well in the sinister tranquillity of summer during the First World War. When we were back in London, Julian Green wished to see the Crystal Palace, and off we drove one afternoon to look at it. The sky was of grey flannel — it was early in March — the air was raw, and the palace, though open, was deserted. It ought to have been haunted by the glad ghost of Victorian confidence, by the excitement of the wondering millions who had visited it, by the organ recitals and soulful vocalisings and junketing visitors of later years; but though still imposing, those glassy walls held only a cold, dirty, and lugubrious emptiness.

After walking a long way we found a sort of indoor water-garden at one end, in a faintly Moorish enclosure and overlooked by assorted Victorian statues, dead white, with dust in their crevices. In the water were tubs, and in the tubs were funereal aspidistras. A bored, elderly workman in waders was going over the leaves with a nailbrush. Another workman on some steps was resting one foot on the back of a large figure of Diana or somebody, from whose shoulders he was straining to remove epaulettes of accumulated filth. Suddenly his foot went through her plaster thorax into the interior of Diana. Anthony Butts burst out laughing, and so did I. But Julian Green looked gravely at this scene of English life inside one of the great monuments of English architecture. His manner was always cautious. It matched his almost prim and wholly correct appearance, which gave little indication of the sombre and smouldering imagination that had already excited interest in his writings.

I turned to go. I was already thinking of the *Criterion* party which its editor, T. S. Eliot, was giving that night, and at which I should meet far weightier contributors than myself, though I did not think I should feel for any of them quite as much respect and admiration as I felt for the author of *The Waste Land*.

5

Moderately Grand Tour

I SET off with Anthony Butts early in 1930 on a European tour. We were away for the best part of a year. In Paris, to which he was no stranger, we met a number of American expatriates of the so-called 'lost generation'. Perhaps they were not representative, but those we met seemed prosperous and self-possessed. From Poussin to Picasso, I looked at a great many pictures, and in between times soon came to understand how easily Paris can attract alien as well as native allegiance.

At Bonn we had the pleasure of getting to know Ernst Robert Curtius, to whom I had an introduction. Of this learned and weighty critic, who seemed as deeply understanding of French as he was of German literature, André Gide had written three years earlier, 'Je trouve en lui, dans son regard, dans le ton de sa voix, dans ses gestes, une douceur, une aménité, une bonté comme évangeliques . . .' His and his wife's kindness and hospitality to us mingled happily with other impressions to give an insight into some lasting aspects of German life. The unruffled Rhine, the pink-flowering chestnuts, the calm walls of the Bishop's palace, the well-kept gardens and houses made an outward harmony, but conversation with university students showed uneasiness and uncertainty. If any reminder were needed that harmony is not easily won, there it was, in a collection of nightmarish shapes—the devices with which Beethoven had tried to conquer deafness.

Moderately Grand Tour

In Berlin we were plunged into the feverish atmosphere that preceded the dominance of Hitler. It was the world upon which our friend Christopher Isherwood was already beginning to focus his camera-eye. Acute political and economic uncertainty and tension was not concealed by the flashy up-to-dateness of life in the centre of the city. Naked ambition and naked despair were both conspicuous. Two strong currents, often intermingling in a puzzling way, especially puzzling to someone unfamiliar with the German character, were earnestness and cynicism. And resentment was visibly gaining over disillusionment.

The atmosphere was certainly stimulating — much too stimulating to be healthy or lasting. The kind of cleverness which, in the Twenties, had produced that surprising periodical the *Querschnitt* was much in evidence, and the then notorious night life was something well worth seeing. Blatant impudicity on such a scale was certainly exciting to youthful senses, but there was something desperately sad about it — and at times something grotesquely funny.

Conscientiously going the rounds of private and public entertainment, of picture gallery and *Nachtlokal*, whom should we encounter but Gide himself, apparently taking his pleasures with his usual seriousness. There is a rather obscure entry in his *Journal* at this time, about hoping to wake up and find himself somebody else, and about hoping to find a new country at the end of a long tunnel. More explicit, in the same month and place, is his saying 'Je voudrais déguster cet été fleur à fleur, comme si ce devait être pour moi le dernier.' Substituting 'premier' for 'dernier', I could have said the same myself.

At Verona we saw Ezra Pound and his father. Coatless and in braces, the father was haranguing the son with an evident consciousness of knowing best which strongly resembled the manner of some of the son's more polemical writings. We had already spent a day or two in Milan, but it was at Verona that I first felt that veneration for the splendour and antiquity of Italy which northerly barbarians are expected to feel. It can be an exalted and yet physical sensation, in which consciousness of the past, sensitiveness to atmosphere, and the sight of the perfect proportions of ancient monuments are made more actual by bland sunlight, by food and wine, by the looks and manners of the people, inheritors of so tremendous a tradition of enlightenment and humanity.

It was too early in the year for Venice to be thronged, but already the water at the Lido was like warm saliva, cigar butts were floating on it here and there, and through the open windows of a large hotel came the African rhythms of a thé dansant. An hour in those surroundings was enough: the rest of our days and nights were given up to the splendours and surprises of the city, of which many aspects were so familiar from painted, photographed, and written images that one had the feeling of returning there, not of being there for the first time. The great monuments of Western civilization, like those of any other, are part of the consciousness of those who have been born into it.

And so to Athens. If I had a son or daughter just grown up, and if either had a suitably responsive or impressionable nature, it would be my wish that he or she should spend a year in Italy and a year in Greece, with as much freedom as possible. I would like my child not only to pay attention to works of art and to mix with educated people, but to get to know some uneducated people or peasants. My hope would be that emotions would be awakened while knowledge was being extended, and that the influence of climate and culture would be heightened by feelings of tenderness as well as of excitement. I should hope that in Italy it might be

Moderately Grand Tour

possible to learn what Dante meant by the expression *anima cortese*, and to appreciate the tactile sense of this nation of artists and craftsmen. And I should look to the dry, white light of Attica to burn away any lingering shreds in my child's mind of puritanical or suburban British fog. It is easy, of course, to be sentimental about Latin or Mediterranean countries: a writer in *The Times Literary Supplement* lately made some sharp comments on the canting ecstasies of travel writers about Greece; even the Parthenon, he said, had become a 'howling cliché'. But there are other things in Athens besides the Parthenon. Some contact with good society in a small capital might be instructive as well as pleasant. Being more compact than in London, Paris, or New York, such a society can be more easily understood; and the conventionality, passions, intrigues, illusions, eccentricities, and scepticism observable in Athenian society could no doubt still arouse, as they aroused in us, liking and admiration as well as amusement.

While in Greece we sought no contacts with anybody but Greeks. There was therefore a language problem. Educated Greeks spoke English or French, but we did not spend all our time with educated Greeks, who were sometimes shocked by our glib use of some low colloquialism we had picked up in unrespectable surroundings. Unless one is a linguist it is necessary in one's travels to employ interpreters or struggle with phrase books. I have always remembered a sentence that occurred in an elementary manual of conversation which I used in Japan: 'Is this purple pencil convenient?' Not really a thing one would often want to say. And there is a wonderful sentence in a nineteenth century phrase book for English travellers in Portugal, or Portuguese travellers in England: 'Bring me a wand and some hooks, I wish to angle.' As I had 'done' Greek for a year or two at school, and as Anthony Butts had been in Greece before, we managed fairly well in a simple way, but when we were together and in need of some particular colloquial phrase, our little book used to fall open at the sentence 'She is always well dressed.' When we wanted to inquire about a journey to Mistra, we found 'Are their nieces tired?' And trying to work out a complaint to a laundry we came upon 'If you had heard Mrs B. you would almost have fainted with delight.'

One afternoon we heard a phrase in English which I have never seen in any manual of conversation, though it might have its uses. We sat down at a café table in the Syntagma, the central square of the city, just as a convoy of cars drove up and off-loaded a swarm of dusty and sweating tourists from the Middle West. *Study Tours in Bible Lands* said a label on each windscreen, and the inquiring pilgrims, footsore, thirsty, and querulous, came swarming into the café. To see the waiter (who knew us) taking our order and making them wait their turn was too much for a formidable matron among them, and in raucous accents which seemed addressed to Providence itself she cried, '*Can't* they wait till their betters are served?'

I should hope that my offspring would have enough imagination to try and see how life might look to American tourists as well as to Greeks, and that a sustained effort would remove whatever vestiges might remain of insular complacency or arrogance —but not that it would weaken the proper pride that may be taken in being English. I should not wish him to think that his forefathers had all wasted their time. And I would wish the young creature to feel something approaching the acute pleasure I myself felt in Greece in my twenties. Alas for the fantasies of parents! Their children are not made in their own image.

Acute pleasure can hardly be described. A little before midday on a morning in early summer I was swimming a good way out in the bay of Phaleron with an inhabitant of Athens of my own age with whose physical beauty I had become infatuated. In the warm sun and the light breeze a small boat with a sail came gliding and prancing past. In it was an old fisherman. When he saw us he asked if we would like to climb in for a sail with him. We said yes, climbed in, and settled down, and while he guided the lightly dancing boat over the sparkling wavelets and glanced back at us now and then with the fatherly playfulness of an old triton, we happily embraced one another with naked arms that the sun had quickly dried, and kissed the saltiness from one another's smiling lips. This, I thought, is happiness — to be young, to be healthy, to be free, to love and be loved in the sun, in the radiant light, flying along over the water in the flawless visibility of early summer in the Aegean.

> What hour shall Fate in all the future find,
> Or what delights, ever to equal these:
> Only to taste the warmth, the light, the wind,
> Only to be alive, and feel that life is sweet?

Neither in sentiment nor in diction are those lines of Binyon's of a kind at all fashionable nowadays, and fault can rightly be found with them; but they do at least hint at the intensity of those moments when one is not 'warming both hands before the fire of life' but conscious of being a flame in the fire itself. I felt a kind of amazement that life could rise to such a pitch, that circumstances could combine to produce and sustain for more than a moment, such perfection.

After a time our lives in Athens took on a certain regularity. Anthony Butts was painting seriously; I had begun to write a book. Both in our working time and our leisure time we led

At Home

independent existences, though living under the same roof. In the mornings I usually put on black spectacles and sat writing out of doors, on a seat in a secluded corner of the Zappeion Gardens. We generally lunched together. During the siesta I was not always alone. In a high white room, shuttered against the heat of an Athenian afternoon in July and against a fine view of the 'howling cliché', the flame that had sprung up in the Bay of Phaleron was often rekindled, while no sound was heard except the plaintive voice of a hawker below in the burning street chanting, in that sad, haunting, but tempting tone of street cries in many parts of the world, the cool, sweet names of melons, grapes, and fresh figs:

'Πεπόνια! Σταφύλια! Συκα φρέσκα!'

Late in the afternoon, or sometimes in the morning, we went off to Glyphada or Vouliagmeni to swim and then to come out and sit in the sun and drink retsina under the pine trees. The colour and salinity of the sea, the piny fragrance of the shadows and the piny tang of the wine, the clearness of the wine and of the white-wine-coloured sea water, the salty warmth of the skin and of the blood, the warmth of the sun and of the sand all seemed interfused, as if the elements of earth, air, fire, and water were one element, in which life was immortal. As often in those parts, a sensuous experience of a certain complexity seemed also a spiritual or at least a suprasensory experience.

Late one afternoon we came back to Athens in a country bus, in which we noticed a peasant pair—the woman for her Madonna-like placidity and regularity of feature, the man for his fierce, bristly, brigand-like aspect. The man took no notice of his wife. In one hand he held a white carnation and on his lap a white rabbit. From time to time, alternately and unselfconsciously, he would smell the carnation and kiss the rabbit, to which he murmured endearments. The mixture of fierceness and gentleness seemed essentially Greek, and more manly than the assumed 'toughness' so common (in every sense of the word) among the English and the Americans.

In the evening, when the Zappeion Gardens, where I had been almost alone in the morning, became exceedingly animated, I was busy seeing, at various levels and as opportunity offered, what can only be called life. To dine late out of doors, outside a restaurant or at some hospitable villa at Psychiko, or in some simple resort by the sea; to see something of night life of the obscurer sort in the Piraeus; to sit late in an alcove of oleanders in the warm semi-darkness and buy sprays of strong-smelling white jasmine from an old woman with a basket; to be alone with that one other person very late, when there was velvet silence and a moon, and soft dust among the rocks, and a consciousness of very old surfaces of marble, and of layers of lost secrets stratified in the air of Attica for two or three thousand years, was to be as if under the unimaginably agreeable influence of a drug.

Lotos-eating, if that is what I was doing, did not keep me from working. I wrote with concentration, as a rule for several hours a day. I had come to a point where, in my myth-making, I was impelled to try and resolve some of the conflicts and harmonize some of the contrasts of my dispersed earlier years. What happens when a child does not grow up in a settled surrounding, in a fixed home, in the bosom of its own family, and constantly surrounded by other families of the same race, class, tradition, and habits as its own? When it finds itself controlled, cherished, or ignored by various kinds of grown-ups of differing social backgrounds, beliefs, and habits? When it has been involved in a series of disjointed contacts with different worlds, like scenes from different plays made to succeed one another but not composing a single play? It is likely to have been over-stimulated and unsettled. It will have learnt in some ways too much, too soon, and too superficially. Precocious and independent in some ways, it will be backward and unsure of itself in others, because is has missed the steadying, ripening effect of a fixed environment, a single tradition, and a homogeneous society. It may resemble a plant too often transplanted, putting out what flowers it can while it can. From such a child I was still evolving, and in the fiction I was trying to compose I was being too ambitious, straining such talent as I possessed, and aiming at something beyond my scope. I had miscalculated—but did not yet know it.

I thought my work was going well, I felt happy in my environment, and it was possible to see something more of it than Athens itself. 'Vous aurez beaucoup de figues,' said an Athenian lady who, like a number of our acquaintances, seemed a Firbankian character. She had a villa on the island of Spetsai and had suggested we should take it for a time: the figs were a symbol of plenty, to go with the envisaged peace. We voyaged there, by way of Hydra, but Athens drew us back.

Greece was for the time being a republic. I forget why, if I ever knew. It is a weakness of the Greeks to get excited about their politics, but they failed to excite me. Voluble explanations about Venizelos or the Bulgarians, delivered with equal energy and variety of gesture at two o'clock in the morning as at two o'clock in the afternoon, seemed to me as much a national failing as English conversations about runs, wickets, and batsmen. I said I was a monarchist and complained because Athens was not more Byzantine, but that only led to protests and fuller, much fuller, explanations. Part of the Royal Palace was open to the public. It lacked magnificence, but the monarchy had not been affluent.

Moderately Grand Tour

Such things as a faded enlargement in a bamboo Oxford frame of a snapshot of Queen Alexandra gave one little more than a feeling of intruding upon the always precarious privacy of royal persons. Nor did I much like it when a charwoman in the Royal Chapel, anxious to explain things to us and no doubt hoping for a tip, picked up the nuptial crown used at weddings and held it over her own head to demonstrate its use. She was only being playful, but the gesture was too much like the playfulness of a tricoteuse.

I do not know if there was any truth in the following story. It was said that when King George and Queen Elizabeth of the Hellenes were still on the throne they had been visited at the Palace of Tatoi, outside Athens, by an American lady. The visitor was so much pestered by flies and other insects that she asked her host and hostess if she might send them some insecticides, squirts, powders, mosquito nets, etc., from America, so that they could get rid of the nuisance. They said they would be pleased. But when she got back to America the lady found there would be various difficulties about sending off the things, so she wrote and suggested that they should be bought in Europe, and enclosed a cheque for $5000. This offering was received at a moment when the Royal funds were low—twenty-four hours, in fact, before the revolution—and it enabled the royal pair to get away. Flit-money, so to speak.

If one is conscious of intense happiness, one is a fool to trust it. Anthony Butts and I received different and unexpected kinds of bad news from England. We could do no good by returning there at once, but in the autumn we began to move westwards. We spent some weeks in Corfu, where we were conscious of a more recent past than in Athens. There were many charming vestiges of the English occupation of the Ionian Islands in the nineteenth century, and we were taken to see the Achilleion by a man formerly attached to the Empress Elizabeth of Austria, whose refuge it had been—so far as there was any refuge from such a destiny as hers.

Anthony Butts painted two or three landscapes of solitary places with ruins or very old buildings, the weather was sultry and still, and huge accumulations of thunderclouds hung in the afternoons over the mountains of Epirus and Albania. One morning we returned to the town in an open carriage by an unfamiliar road which passed for a time between two cactus hedges. Then there was an open space and not far from the road a whitewashed cabin by itself. The door was partly concealed by a rustic pergola entirely covered with a profusion of convolvulus in flower, in many different colours. A girl in a red skirt appeared in the doorway, and a young man in a white shirt standing under the pergola looked over his shoulder at us as we went by. It happened that my friend had a very strong liking, almost a mania, for convolvulus, and he at once said he must paint the scene, which was strikingly beautiful. We arranged to come back the next morning, but when we did come back there was no trace of the house, or the flowers, or the two people—simply an open space. It was not only disappointing but disconcerting. The hallucination—if such it was—had been shared by the driver, who was as disquieted as ourselves to find nothing, and I do not know how it can be explained.

Swimming too far out to sea as usual—from habit, not bravado—I narrowly missed bisection by a steamer. I have said that I was not addicted to drink, but I was addicted to water, a craving for which seems to be transmittable from father to son: after all, President Kruger had compared my father to a fish. I was a leisurely and far less accomplished swimmer than my father, and spent far more of my time in the water than he did.

Moderately Grand Tour

I understand now that swimming, and the basking that follows it where climate permits, is a drug—one might almost say a dangerous drug. That agreeable but essentially purposeless movement in another element, away from the world, as it were; that abandonment to muscular rhythm, to the seeming use of all the muscles; and that lulling sensation of well-being that follows, with the nerves comforted and the mental processes subdued, are all part of what moralists might call an escape. Water being a feminine element, probably to swim in it means that one is trying to return to the womb. I make no excuses; even if my addiction to swimming showed a weak or retarded character, I enjoyed every moment of it.

I had been reading a good deal about the Greek War of Independence, and in Corfu I saw a painting of the Suliot women about to throw themselves and their offspring over a precipice rather than fall into the clutches of the tyrant, Ali Pasha. It was only an anecdotal painting of no great merit, but the image so haunted me that a few years later I wrote his life. After it was published I was reading a story by Balzac and found that he had written these words: 'Allez, Ali, pacha de Jannina, est un homme incompris, il lui faudrait un historien.' As I had no pretensions to being an historian, it was perhaps forward of me to attempt such a book, but it has been tolerantly and even kindly spoken of by professional historians. As they sometimes seem to be members of a narrow and exclusive sect, favourable notice of an outsider or amateur seems quite a trophy. The theme seemed to me to have a certain topicality: the book is in fact an account of a dictator's misuse of power, and it attempts to show how a cruel monster can exert charm and can seem both execrable and likeable—to some.

One afternoon in Corfu, Anthony Butts and I were having a drink in the house of a Corfiote lady. Somehow or other he had

launched into a scandalous satirical tirade against Mussolini. It
was extremely funny. Before it was done the lady, who seemed
'not amused', leaned sideways in rather a strained attitude and
raised one finger to point over her shoulder. Immediately behind
her was a large signed photograph of that distasteful individual,
floridly inscribed by him to herself. It was an abrupt reminder
that we were in the Thirties now.

6

The Good Sir Hugh

A<small>T</small> intervals in my life I have been drawn towards South
Wales and the Border Country, to the landscape and some
of the people there. As a boy I had spent an idyllic summer with my friend Bob Synge at Cwmbach, the home of his
family in Radnorshire. And now I felt drawn in that direction
again: I wanted to be alone in the country and get on with my
work. I spent a winter at Lingen in Herefordshire, staying at the
inn, where I was made comfortable by a friendly family. I was
able to write in peace, and to explore on foot the region round
Knighton and Presteigne. In those days there was hardly any
traffic on the less important roads, and walking made it possible
to enjoy country details and casual encounters. In a country place
characters emerged 'in the round' and in variety. If I had been less
occupied, I might have wished that I had been born and bred in
such a place, where everybody knew or knew about one another,
and felt their roots entwined.

When my book was finished I went to live in Pimlico, where
nobody had roots. While there I discovered that the book did not
form a proper unity: it remained episodic. Some parts were the
result of a truly creative process; everything between them, everything that was supposed to hold them together, seemed mere contrivance. The discovery did not make me dejected. I was relieved
to be able to see (with the help of a total stranger from America)
how and where I had failed. There was no sense of wasted time or

effort. I knew there were good things in the book, and saw that some of them, rewritten, could stand by themselves. I rewrote them, and they stood by themselves, and appeared in print as short stories, or as what are so oddly called long short stories. These were thought well of by persons whose opinions I most cared for.

There must always be a gap between the imaginative writer and the reader. The writer, if he is any good, is working out a new interpretation of life; the reader holds a variety of accepted ideas. Collaboration between them is not always easy: it may take a long time to be possible. A taste for the work of any original artist is an acquired taste. Goethe speaks somewhere of how one often takes no pleasure in a work of art at first sight, because it is too strange. But by trying to perceive its merits one may discover new faculties in oneself. He says that an artist can show no greater respect for his public than by never bringing it what it expects, but what he himself thinks right and proper in that stage of his own and others' culture in which he finds himself. But what was my public, and where exactly did I stand in relation to it? When a writer feels he does not belong wholly to the environment to which he chiefly belongs—in my case, England—as he would if he had never left it when young, uncertainties must arise in his mind. Early experiences elsewhere will have made him still more unlike his potential public than he would have been in any case. His own view of life will certainly differ more from that accepted unquestioningly for the most part by most of that public: his very subject matter, by its remoteness, may be not only strange but with little or no appeal to them. Among the things that had aroused me most and found expression in my earlier writings had been racial conflicts in South Africa and the duality, or divided nature, of the Japanese. However lacking in weight or ripeness those writings had been, they had contained clear foreseeings of such things as the intensifying of the racial crisis in South Africa, and the intensifying of racial fanaticism and militarism in Japan. How could I expect English readers then to know or care about these things, though they were to me of great urgency? And how could I now understand the stage of my own and others' culture, or estimate the width of the gap between them?

Chance brought me into contact with a popular novelist for whom no such gap appeared to exist, and it was interesting to learn something of the workings of such a writer. At Tavistock Square one evening I was surprised to be introduced to Hugh Walpole. I wondered what he was doing there. I had read one or two of his early books but had felt little or no curiosity about their author. I now saw before me a pink, portly, restless man who seemed to be enjoying himself but on the defensive—which was not surprising, because Virginia Woolf was teasing him. He made himself agreeable to me, and when we were leaving invited me to lunch. I accepted the invitation. I did not then know two things that are plainly shown in my old friend Rupert Hart-Davis's admirable life of him: that he was an untiring encourager of any indications of talent in writers younger than himself, and that his life was not just a quest for a perfect friend but for any number of perfect friends. To be a perfect friend to anybody would be difficult, and much as I came to like Hugh Walpole and to have reason to be grateful to him, I never felt myself destined to intimate or confidential acquaintance with him. Nor did I feel easy in his company: it was no good being oneself, because the romantic novelist in him saw one as somebody very different, whom one was neither able nor willing to impersonate.

When in London, Hugh Walpole occupied a first floor above Piccadilly. The entrance was just round the corner in Half Moon

At Home

Street; and from his high french windows there was a view down an avenue in the Green Park towards the Victoria Memorial. So central a situation seemed fitting for him. His flat seemed like the setting for a character in one of his novels; he himself was more like a character in a novel by somebody else. A keen acquirer, he at once showed me some of the latest things he had bought—a rare and ancient book, a modern bronze figure, a jade carving, a Sickert, a Renoir. I was the only guest, and the interest he expressed in my writing was obviously more real than that of a politely affable host. When he said, 'What are you writing now?' I told him that I had just scrapped a long novel I had been working on for some time. His reply is recorded in Rupert Hart-Davis's biography; I repeat it here.

'Marvellous, marvellous! What courage! *I've* never had the courage to destroy anything!' Then, after a pause, 'Do you know, you make me feel just like a little girl taken to see the elephants for the first time.'

I did not know him well enough to be sure whether he was being ironical or not. I had not thought it an act of courage to do away with the novel, but hoped it was a sign of improving judgment. Because Hugh Walpole himself wrote with facility he was apt to be fascinated by the hesitations of writers less fluent and less sanguine than himself. I, for my part, was astonished to see a popular writer at close quarters. In a book of reminiscences called *The Apple Trees* he has told how he deliberately put into his first novel 'everything that would, I hoped, help it. Cornish scenery of a very coloured kind, a noble long-suffering hero, a beautiful heroine, a female sinner who repented, a theme apposite to the day.' I think he went on writing as easily as he had begun because he knew precisely, by instinct, what the large and not acutely critical public he wrote for would like. People were sometimes irritated by his ebullience and air of assurance, but he was more understanding of his own weaknesses than he appeared. His pen would race ahead, he hardly ever paused to make a correction, he never destroyed what he had written, but, he told me, the buoyant optimism he felt about whatever book he was writing, *while* he was writing it, was liable to collapse as soon as he had finished it, and to give way to doubts. If those doubts had been stronger, or had set in sooner, he would have written fewer books, and his books might have had smaller circulations and more serious appraisal than they have had. If I, on the other hand, had had fewer doubts and a tenth of Hugh Walpole's fluency, I should have written more and oftener and been better off and better known than I am. Not that I have anything to complain about in the responses my writings have met with.

'There's one thing I *have* got,' he would say defensively, as if one was about to attack him. 'I *have* got the narrative gift, I *can* tell a story.'

He was quite right. His gift for inventive narrative was quite out of the ordinary. A Balzac without copiousness would not have been Balzac; but here was copiousness without Balzac, and this was Walpole. His understanding was acute enough to enable him to see that his gifts as a novelist were incomplete, and behind his air of assurance was a most uneasy awareness of the fact, and an uncommon vulnerability.

His little joke about the elephants was not without point: if he had called me a rogue elephant, it might have had even more, because he was speaking to someone rather deficient in the herd instinct. A nomadic early life may make a man inured to a certain independence, yet adaptable enough to attach himself now to this herd, now to that, as opportunity offers or occasion or inclination demand. If a novelist, he is likely to be of an eccentric, marginal, or occasional kind. To produce a large or solid body of work, even today, it still seems necessary for a novelist to have and enjoy an essentially uninterrupted relation to one background and the environment of his earliest years — like Hugh Walpole. Otherwise one can only expect his novels to be few and spasmodic, the product of some special stimulus or phase of development.

These indications of the difference between Hugh Walpole and myself are confirmed in a report on a manuscript of mine which I saw some years later. It was written by Edward Garnett. After a statement which modesty prevents my repeating, he wrote:

> Plomer is emphatically of the minority, i.e. of the section of writers, the real intelligentsia, the unconventional, critical-minded, literary artists whom the British Public in general don't *like*, and therefore only buy in restricted quantities. He is a Left-winger in popularity, i.e. what D. H. Lawrence was to Hugh Walpole.

If this was true, then all the more credit to Hugh Walpole for doing all that he did to help and encourage creatures of the same species as myself. But patronage and encouragement of writers and artists do not necessarily make those who exert them liked or respected, especially if they are envied for their position, their success, or their fortune. Their hands are liable to become deeply indented with scars caused by bites from those they have fed. In the case of Hugh Walpole, his enthusiasm (with which, as he once wrote, he 'always had trouble'), his excitability over manifestations of creativeness, his longing to be liked and to attach people and things to himself, did *seem* to make him undiscriminating. It would be truer, as well as kinder, to say that he was eclectic. If his abode at 90 Piccadilly, had a somewhat museum-like aspect, the various things in it had been chosen because he liked them as examples of their kind. It was well known that he was a keen amasser of pictures, books, other works or objects of art, and bibelots, and his enemies said that he was gullible and that his gullibility was taken advantage of by sharp dealers and anti-quaries in Bond Street and elsewhere. But when his collection of pictures was shown after his death these same traducers were sur-prised to see that he had either been well advised, or had shown a flair, or both, because he had often bought remarkably good and sometimes surprising examples of the work of some great painters and some interesting or neglected ones. Similarly, though his range of acquaintance was extremely wide, I have never known or known of anybody he liked who was without some dis-tinction of character. Some persons who were fond of him were of the utmost distinction: to have won in early life, and not to have lost, the affection of Henry James was no common thing.

Hugh Walpole had tendencies observable in other best-selling writers. However successful, popular, and prosperous, and how-ever confident of undiminished ability to continue so, such writers incline, even more than other writers with more obvious cause, to be touchy and uneasy. They seldom seem as contented with their success as might be expected. Not only their talents, ambition, and hard work have made them successful, but their pandering to the accepted ideas, romantic sentimentality, stupid prejudices, and complacent woollenheadedness of mediocrity in the mass, their willingness to put into their work 'everything that would help it', or some 'theme apposite to the day'. It seems un-reasonable, therefore, that they should feel injured because they have failed to receive the praise of those not necessarily choicer but 'choosier' spirits who by their nature must always be in a minority. Yet they do. Their vanity is wounded—and an author's vanity, as Chekhov wrote, is 'vindictive, implacable, incapable of for-giveness'. (About Chekhov, be it remembered, there was nothing wistful or dreamy: as Shestov wrote, he had a 'pitiless talent'.) In those ostensibly 'normal', breezy, man-to-man types a form of persecution mania is apt to germinate. They imagine themselves to be the victims of conspiracies either of silence or of denigration among persons or (often imaginary) coteries who are simply not interested in them. They are then in danger of adopting a scornful attitude against highbrows or aesthetics or eggheads (or whatever the current term of abuse happens to be for those who seem to qualify for it), complain that they are stuck-up, or precious, or out of touch with 'ordinary' people (meaning their own public) or with the events 'apposite to the day'. But when some favour-able notice is taken of them by these despised beings they are apt to go abruptly into reverse.

When secretly tormented by a knowledge or a suspicion of their own limitations—like a stone in the shoe, or an ant in the pants—it is surely because they do not accept that it is their own limitations that have made them what they are. They want to have their cake and eat other people's too. Even Hugh Walpole was not without this appetite. Only a mean spirit could have grudged him his pleasure in making a great deal of money and spending it in ways he enjoyed or upon objects he coveted. But he did seem a little inconsistent when, for instance, at one moment he would express a laughable anxiety lest the current sales of his latest book might be surpassed by the latest book of Brett Young, a then successful writer of popular fiction; and at the next moment show acute anxiety to please somebody more concerned with matters of taste than those of circulation.

The fact that Hugh Walpole had a kind of veneration for Virginia Woolf and was constantly anxious to write something

she might approve of was in itself evidence that he was not entirely complacent about his own writings. There was something
winning about his anxiety to please. She teased him, and since we
do not bother to tease people unless we like them, she obviously
felt a kind of affection for him. I think she was fascinated by his
energy, by the way he lived and worked, and by the candour with
which he could, to a sympathetic listener, talk about his own
experience or people he had known, revelling as he did so in a
freedom, a plain speaking, he could never allow himself in
addressing his public.

If tape recordings had been as easy then as they are now, I
would have tried to persuade him to record some of the stories he
had to tell. They were sometimes scandalous, but none the duller
for that; and he told them with a lively humour and a kind of
worldly scepticism that are not, I think, conspicuous in his books.
I remember particularly an extraordinary account of a visit paid
to Conrad by Robert Hichens, accompanied by an intimate
friend who was male, large in body, a cook by vocation, and
Russian by nationality. The radar-like sensitivity of Conrad to the
intrusion into his domestic sphere of a Russian became even more
agitated by what seemed to him the social solecism of causing it
and by his instantaneous suspicion of what seemed to him an
equivocal relationship; and the combustion set up in the great man
by the duties of a host, the prejudices of a Pole, and the antipathy
of a heterosexual almost caused him to explode. Mrs Conrad, a
faithful pourer of oil upon waters more often troubled than not,
found on this occasion that all her years of practice were of very
little help. It is sad to think what golden harvests of scandal are
lost because the reapers do not, for various reasons, record them.
And it is pleasant to think that Hugh Walpole was once kissed in
public by Conrad, who recorded in writing his feeling that

At Home

thanks were due to a 'Higher Power' for the friendship of which that was a token. The man who won that tribute is not to be written off as a nonentity or an ass.

A few doors way from 90 Piccadilly was the Ritz, where a man had been pointed out to me as a regular frequenter with an unusual habit. He was what used sometimes to be called a well-groomed man, and of middle age. His thinning white hair was parted in the middle of a symmetrical scalp. There was nothing plethoric about his complexion, which was of a neutral tint. A rather full moustache, in an Omdurman or Majuba style but well cared for, seemed to emphasize the suavity of a face upon which neither a single thought nor a single emotion appeared ever to have pencilled its signature. His head was supported by a starched collar of a height then no longer customary: it might have come from his shirtmaker in 1910. And his shirtmaker, like his tailor and his shoemaker, was probably not far away: he was perfectly dressed, in a style that would have been unobtrusive twenty years earlier, but was by this time dated. His grooming was less interesting than, so to speak, his oats: the story was that he came to lunch alone at the Ritz every day, and having eaten his way through the meal, stopped short of coffee, and ate his way through the same succession of courses a second time. This was a solemn thought. Whether he was actuated by appetite or gluttony, the thought of, say, a meringue with an extra dollop of whipped cream being followed by turtle soup, and of another similarly enriched meringue rising into view beyond the second rounds of lobster and jugged hare, was gruesome enough to make one's palate creep.

A few hundred yards eastwards, in Denman Street, there was an inconspicuous basement I had discovered and often visited. In it was a small Greek restaurant where one could be sure of eating well at a proper cost. That is something important for a self-employed young man on his own in London. I remember Dr Pood telling me that in his day he had relied on the cheapness and goodness of one meal a day at a small Chinese restaurant near this very place: it was there perhaps that he had formed his less commendable taste for Brummagem chinoiserie.

Honest Mr Stelios did the cooking himself and would take one into his savorous little kitchen to show what he had in preparation and to guide one's choice. I introduced two or three of my closest friends there, under a strict promise that they would tell nobody else: the place would soon have lost its character if invaded by knowing male and female twitterers from the westwards. That so good, so homely, and so secret an eating place should be almost within arm's length of Piccadilly Circus, and as good as invisible, gave meals there almost the sweet taste of stolen fruit. I remember how pleasing it was one day to notice, hanging from three adjacent hooks on the coat rack that served as a cloakroom, an overcoat, a side of lamb, and a guitar. This Levantine islet was a whole continent away from Pimlico, where many of the floating population seemed [to sustain themselves with clammy oddments out of paper bags and greasy improvisations over a gas ring.

'I do hope you've got nice rooms,' said one of my aunts with affectionate considerateness. She was sitting in her Cotswold garden under a bower of buddleias: on each fat flower two or three velvety peacock butterflies, drugged with the warm odour of honey and the honeyed warmth of the sun, seemed like mounted specimens. There seemed no reason why they should ever move, or why the flowers should ever fade, or my aunt ever grow older or less lively.

'Very, thank you,' I said. It would have seemed somehow

priggish to explain that my 'rooms' amounted to only one, and
that it was no hardship to me to be occupying it. My room might
very well have been a model for one of Sickert's Camden Town
interiors. Its large brass bedstead would have served equally well
for cheerful nights or hopeless dawns, and no doubt the shining
metal globes with which it was ornamented had reflected in their
time a variety of domestic tragedies and comedies, like tiny
scenes cut from a lost film, scenes that had been more amply
reflected in the large and mottled Victorian mirror with the
carved frame over the fireplace. To this succession of little dramas
I had visitors who contributed. Of special interest to me just
then was the table, covered with a mohair cloth in spinach green,
upon which I was writing a novel based upon the misfortunes of
Mrs Fernandez, *The Case is Altered*.

If I had been obliged by illness or some other cause to spend all
my time in this phrontistery, or if I had felt it to be more than a
temporary expedient, I might have felt gloomy, but I doubt it.
In fact I found it intensely interesting. To live in such an environment was quite new to me, and what I observed of the life of the
quarter began to excite my curiosity about some of the many
Londons unknown to me. I had already seen enough to understand that there were many survivals not only in architecture
and furniture, but in the ways of life of some of the inhabitants,
from Victorian and even from Dickensian London. I have never
understood the term 'ordinary people', and I could see then that
there was quite as much eccentricity at lower economic and social
levels as in Mayfair or Bloomsbury or Bayswater. And what of the
vast unexplored tracts of London extending in all directions? I
longed to know more about the lives that went on in them and
was to be found sampling the life of Islington or the Elephant
and Castle.

The Good Sir Hugh

Poverty is easily supportable when it is not a whole-time occupation and one is young and active. If I was going out to dinner and wanted a bath beforehand, I had to go to the public baths, because there was no bathroom in the house where I was living and I did not care to sponge either at or on my friends. My only regret was that public baths in England were not sociable as in Japan, but solitary.

Moving on various social levels, I was learning and enjoying much, and becoming more acclimatized again to London and to English life, but my interests and connections were too diverse to be harmonized. A constructive life implies a tying together of loose ends, but mine were so many and various that the knots themselves tended to be peculiar.

A little later on, when Peter Davies asked me to contribute to his pioneer series of short biographies a life of Cecil Rhodes, I readily agreed. I felt that I had the right to attempt to define Rhodes' character and career in terms which would have been impossible at an earlier date and which, though not likely to be popular, would be in keeping with my conviction that Africa in the future was likely to prove something more than the sterling area of his fancies. It already seemed urgent that the West should pay more attention to deserving goodwill than to annexing territory. I said in the introduction to the book that I did not intend either to try and prove Rhodes a scoundrel or 'to affect a gross impartiality'. The book pleased and annoyed exactly the persons, or kinds of persons, I expected it to please or annoy. On completing it, I had decided to dedicate it to Hugh Walpole. This was a chance to pay him a compliment in public, and, as he was a collector of such things, I presented him with the manuscript. But what an odd conjunction of names! Although Rhodes was a hero to many of Walpole's public, I think the novelist himself can have had little or no interest in the subject, and the book itself could only, in those now far-off days, have been regarded as almost subversive or at least outrageous by the more jingoistic old memsahibs in the circulating libraries of Truro or Tunbridge Wells. Can there have been in the dedicator, besides a genuine wish to pay a compliment, just a suggestion of mischievousness?

7

The Shield of Achilles

A CHANGE in the fortunes both of Anthony Butts and myself decided us to set up and share the expenses of a joint establishment in London where he could paint and I could write, and where we could entertain our friends — who were not always friends of both of us. We found a house we liked, one of those old white houses in Canning Place, off Palace Gate. It was in good condition, quiet, and not cut off from the sun; it had room for us both to pursue co-existence without clashing; and the garden had been occupied once and for all by a single species of wild flower. Beneath the sour London soil its roots proliferated like an inexhaustible supply of half-cooked spaghetti, and in the summer the leaves swarmed up and mantled everything, putting out a vast number of large flowers: it was a white convolvulus. And far from attempting to extirpate it, we gave it every encouragement, as if to make up for the Corfiot mirage.

I have twice mentioned Walter Sickert. He told me that Anthony Butts was the best talker he had heard since Degas. They had known one another for some time, and used to have tremendous jokes together. For a time my friend became Sickert's pupil, though I think without much benefit to his painting. His natural inclination was towards a smooth and thickish impasto, a Courbet-like sumptuousness, and the squared-up canvases he prepared in the Sickert manner and began to cover patchily with thin paint came to nothing. His inclination was to something more

monumental than the translated photographs of Victorian variations, however brilliant, of the later Sickert.

I seem to remember that one of the Georgian poets wrote some
painfully winsome verses expressing gratification at having heard
a cuckoo while looking at a rainbow. His pleasure cannot have
been so rare as ours at the synchronized presence one evening in
our little drawing room of Walter Sickert and Lady Ottoline
Morrell. I should hesitate to say which was the cuckoo and which
the rainbow, and it may have been by contrivance and not by
chance that they came together under our roof. It was an evening
worth more than all the collected and combined poems of
Geoffrey Smallbeer and Roland Milk.

Our two guests got on like a house on fire. After a time they
began swapping recollections of the music halls, and became so
enkindled that they rose to their feet and performed from
memory a music-hall turn, with a pas de deux and a duet.
Neither was young, so their animation was the more glorious.
Sickert, wearing a Harris tweed frock-coat with trousers to
match, and doeskin spats, held out his arms to Lady Ottoline and
performed what was almost a series of high kicks. She, strikingly
dressed as usual, with a flying scarf of flame-coloured chiffon,
jingling ornaments, and hoop-like earrings, held out her long
arms to him and repeatedly raised and extended a stork-like leg
until it was almost parallel with the ground. And together they
sang, or rather declaimed, with tremendous gusto and emphasis:

> I *throw* my affection
> In *your* direction,
> You're just my size and style!

'Le fond du caractère anglais,' according to Taine, 'c'est l'absence
de bonheur.' I wonder.

The Shield of Achilles

Another of our visitors at Canning Place was Christopher Isherwood. He was a letter writer of exceptional brilliance, and when he moved on from Berlin, original observations made in Copenhagen, in Lisbon, or later from China (literally, as they say) to Peru, arrived in a very small, regular, and evidently imperturbable handwriting. If, as he pretended, he was a sort of camera eye, then the eye of no camera can ever have had a more diamond-like twinkle in it. And when he appeared in person, his conversation continued in exactly the same tone as his letters. 'Amazing' was one of his favourite words, and his capacity to be amazed by the behaviour of the human species, so recklessly displayed everywhere, made him a most entertaining talker. I have an impression that the young, or youngish, English intellectuals in those days were, when high spirited, somehow freer in their high spirits than the conscientious and understandably troubled ones of today, who seem much concerned with what was called in Victorian times mutual improvement. Christopher Isherwood, compactly built, with his commanding nose, Hitlerian lock of straight fair hair falling over one bright eye, and the other looking equally bright under a bristly eyebrow already inclined to beetle, an expression of amusement in a photo-finish with an expression of amazement as he came to the conclusion of a story, and almost choking with delight at the climax, also made Taine look silly — or would have done so, if one had been thinking of him.

And then there was Nancy Cunard. Arriving slender and trim on a piercing day, she peeled off, as she came into the room, onion-like layers of elegance — a close-fitting jerkin of soft suede, then inner skins that seemed wisps of silk or wafers of wool, until she was slenderness's own self, showing a cat-like appreciation of the fire, and turning her steady and uncompromising gaze upon ourselves. Her eyes, like those of some cats, were lucent among their dark lashes, a pale and precious enamel in which had been fused a suggestion of gold dust—a sentient enamel. And when she moved to put a cigarette or cup or glass to her lips, attention was inevitably attracted to her thin, fine-boned arms, both encased in such a concatenation of wide, weighty armlets of rigid African ivory that the least movement produced a clacking sound, as of billiard balls or the casual cakewalk of a skeleton.

Already, with her courage and independence, she made no bones (as we seem to be on that subject), whether in the United States or in Europe, about her complete indifference to the colour bar and her partisanship on behalf of those who were suffering most by it—like the victims of the Scottsboro trial. Anthony Butts had known her for some time and they seemed fond of one another. She had come this time with a particular purpose—to talk about a projected book. Among some old press cuttings of the early thirties I notice this, from a literary weekly:

> Nancy Cunard arrived this week in London from France with the manuscript of her forthcoming anthology *Negro*, which contains 475,000 words and 400 photographs of contemporary Negro personalities. Among her 150 collaborators are Norman Douglas, Augustus John, George Antheil, William Plomer, and Professor Westermarck.

It was an honour to be classed as one of her collaborators, though my own contribution to this impressively conceived and edited book was not a weighty one.

I saw much at this time of Lilian Bowes Lyon, who was a near neighbour, living then in Courtfield Gardens. Her grip on life was intense but always seemed somehow precarious; as it became more precarious it grew more intense, but it was not the grip of rapacity. She had a passionate concern for right relationships between human beings, and it extended far beyond the boundaries of nationality, class, or convention. She had, with it, the instincts and the courage of an artist, and in later life a long fight to the death with prolonged and exceptional physical pain.

She could find no abiding place in this world. In later years I used to go and see her in a succession of temporary homes—in Gloucestershire, in Hertfordshire, in Surrey, at Holmbury St Mary, later at Ham Common, and finally in Brompton Square. My first and last impressions of her (and I believe I was the last person to see her alive) were of her gentleness of manner and intensity of feeling. Her gaze—now withdrawn, now direct and glowing—was without subterfuge. The bones of her face, delicate but strong, suggested her firmness of purpose and the fineness with which she exerted it. She spoke with strong emphasis, but always in a very low and pleasing voice. Her firmness was to be needed: though pity and consideration for others were with her always, it was in her own being that fortitude was demanded of her.

Lady Ottoline Morrell, when I introduced them, remarked to her that they were connections. Though very different natures, they had more than a link of blood in common. The younger woman was, in her way, no less unconforming and independent. She had torn herself from her home in Northumberland and a segregated family life (of a nineteenth-century type) to launch out on her own, to live in London as she thought fit, and to write. She produced a novel, which rattled some of her older and less flexible relations, not because it was libellous or indecent or politically tendentious but because it did not conform to their conventions either that she should write, or that she should write fiction, or that, if she did, she should write fiction suggesting that life was not a wholly comfortable proceeding. Her first

novel was not her last: perhaps to spare those objectors from re-
newed vibrations, she put out another under a pseudonym.
Jejune writers about 'the novel' have not understood clearly
enough how often in the inter-war years a novel was the form in
which it was most convenient for young men and women to express and record their consciousness of finding themselves in a
world of changing values. It gave them a chance to challenge or
flout or protest against what seemed to them stale or sterile, and
to advance their own ideas of emancipation, progress, right-
mindedness, or leftwingedness. So far as the vast output of first
novels in that period is concerned, it is probably true to say that
while very few are of enduring literary value a good many are of
some sociological interest. It was, however, in the writing of
poetry that Lilian Bowes Lyon was best able to try and communicate some of the stirrings of her spirit and the complexities or
simplicities of her view of life.

I have always been interested in heredity. On her mother's side
Lilian Bowes Lyon was related to Lady Anne Barnard, who
wrote *Letters from the Cape*, a masterpiece of the early colonial
period of South African literature. And the history of the Earls
of Strathmore is anything but dull, and includes that of *The Unhappy Countess* and her demon lover, so effectively told by Mr
Ralph Arnold in his book of that name.* Augustus Hare, in his
fascinating autobiography *The Story of My Life*, makes much of
his connection with the family. Excessively, even painfully,
class-conscious and cousin-conscious, even by Victorian standards,
he had the virtue of curiosity and collected many anecdotes that
would otherwise have been lost. He gives a pleasing description
of his occasional visits to Ridley Hall on the South Tyne, which
was later the home of Lilian Bowes Lyon. I asked her whether

* Published by Constable, 1957.

she thought his account of the supernatural mysteries at Glamis Castle was to be taken seriously. She told me that very soon after her parents were married her father took his bride to Glamis for the first time. They went there in daylight; he was driving, I think, a dogcart; and she was seated beside him. As they were approaching the castle he was startled to hear her utter a sound of distress. Instantly turning to ask her what was the matter, he pulled up. She had covered her eyes with her hand.

'Oh!' she said, hardly able to speak. 'That poor, poor woman!'

'What woman?'

' There, just there beside the drive! She was running! You must have seen her!'

'I saw nobody,' he said gently. 'There was no woman there. You must have imagined it. What was she like?'

Lady Anne Bowes Lyon could hardly speak, but she said:

'She had such an *agonized* expression on her face. She was running, and holding out both arms in front of her, but —oh!— her hands had been cut off, and the stumps were bleeding!'

'Ah,' said her husband, as if now he understood. 'I didn't see her, but I know about her. I know she has been seen.'

There are other stories or legends of troubled spirits associated with the house, but none so painfully memorable. Atrocities in Scotland in the Middle Ages cannot have been worse than those in England but were no doubt just as bad. Nightmarish visions of desolated or outraged humanity may still appear, lifelike in the dark caves of history; and history is not merely a matter of records, or of records interpreted; those caves are part of the endless underground system of unconscious memory.

I do not wish to suggest that Lilian Bowes Lyon was fey, or preoccupied with the supernatural. She was not remote from this earth, nor from other people, nor from what was going on in countries not her own. A kind of criminal negligence is sometimes attributed by a younger generation to those who were flourishing in the Thirties. That is not surprising: children always think they know better than their parents, and their own children too will be wise after the event and will formulate against them charges of folly, stupidity, mismanagement, and irresponsibility. I should hesitate to say that those who are generally classified as intellectuals would govern better than politicians. They would probably be too reasonable. But if some of my friends were classified as intellectuals, they were none the worse for that. It seems to me that they saw further, sooner, and more clearly than most people, even than most of those whose business it was to look ahead. Before the Twenties were out, Anthony Butts regarded another World War in the near future as a matter of course, and our visit to Germany confirmed him in an opinion that really needed no confirmation. In the early Thirties I would sooner have had a report on Germany from Christopher Isherwood than from Sir Nevile Henderson: fresh from his observation post there, he told me he thought a war between Germany and Poland inevitable. But who would ever have taken any notice of him then, if he had said so in public? Leonard Woolf explained to me that the international situation was a repetition of what it had been some years before 1914, and foretold almost exactly the date of the beginning of the Second World War. But to take such serious views then was to risk being called a crank, a bore, an alarmist, or a defeatist. Stephen Spender, now in Hamburg, now in Vienna, and later in Spain, had gone so far as to adhere to what seemed to him then the only effective opposition to the forces of reaction and oppression. If it was a mistake, it was an honourable mistake.

I did not myself then regard it as an obligation to be involved in politics, to advocate policies, to join parties, and to protest against injustices in every part of the world. For one thing, I was not politically minded. For another, because I had been living when younger in Africa and Japan during the most emotional and impressionable time of my life, their problems were still nearer to me than the confusions and ferocities of Europe. Furthermore, I was chiefly interested in the pursuit of literature and in personal relationships. Also, I was not yet thirty, and my education and even my re-Westernization were far from complete.

I suppose it is a flat truism to say that the greatest force in education is example. There was one visitor to Canning Place whose example and personality aroused an admiration and affection which were immediate and lasting. This was E. M. Forster. Although he had a perching-place in Brunswick Square and seemed to be on good terms with that group of friends and acquaintances whose similarities of social origin, outlook, interest, and habit, to say nothing of early influences at Cambridge, had caused them to be spoken of as 'Bloomsbury', he never seemed to me to be quite one of them. I saw him, and see him, as an independent.

During the years that followed I saw him often and got to know him better than any other writer of his generation. His liveliness, charm, insight, understanding, and unlikeness to anybody else made his friendship the rarest of treasures. In appearance he was the reverse of a dandy. Incurious fellow passengers in a train, seeing him in a cheap cloth cap and a scruffy waterproof, and carrying the sort of little bag that might have been carried in 1890 by the man who came to wind the clocks, might have thought him a dim provincial of settled habits and taken no more notice of him. When I said as much in an essay written during the Second World War for the French review *Fontaine*, published in Algiers, I sent him a copy for his approval or disapproval before it went to the printer. He showed it, or read it, to his mother, who said, 'There! You see what Mr Plomer says. How often have I told you, Morgan dear, that you really ought to brush your coat?'

Crouched in a corner of that imaginary railway compartment, he would have worn a kind of protective colouring, like an oak egger or a stick insect—or, rather, like a retired booking office clerk from a station on a branch line. It can never have been said of him, as it was said of another literary man of my acquaintance, 'Nobody could possibly be as distinguished as X looks.' But one might have said that only an uncommonly distinguished man would have taken so little trouble to look like one. The moment he was engaged in conversation with anybody in the least congenial, or potentially congenial, he lighted up. First the vivacity of his mind became apparent, his openness to new impressions; then some comment, softly yet sharply striking exactly the right note, would seem to be striking the very note that nobody else would have touched upon at that moment; then gradually it might become guessable how his variety of experience and interests had combined with his originality of mind to form his powers of judgment. His is essentially a critical mind.

One did not think of him in terms of age. Recalling him in absence, one thought of certain quick darting movements and bird-like inclinations of the head; of the intense blue of his eye in certain lights, as if it had changed colour; of the sweetness of his smile; of the little puffs and spasms of laughter that rushed out beneath his untidy moustache; and of his real and not officious politeness, his winning considerateness to the shyest and least self-important persons in mixed gatherings. He often varied his surroundings and his company, but no man could be more tenacious of associations once cherished.

Years later, in a book about him, Lionel Trilling was to write that in a world at war E. M. Forster reminded us of a world of true order: 'he is one of those who raise the shield of Achilles, which is the moral intelligence of art, against the panic and emptiness which make their onset when the will is tired from its own excess.' Rose Macaulay, that staunch independent with an impassioned concern for the abolition of cant and for the proper use of words, listed, in her book about Forster, some of the things he believed in and disbelieved in. He believed, she said, in personal relationships, in individuality, in beauty, in affection, in liberty, and in democracy; he disbelieved in nationalism, empire, militarism, catchwords, Christianity, oligarchy, dictatorship, big business, schoolmasters, 'and a number of other things'. And Forster himself, in a pamphlet called *What I Believe*, provided his own explanations. It is a good thing that he did, because it must be said that words like 'beauty', 'liberty', and 'democracy' are elastic: they have been so abused by stretching that what they ought to describe may wrongly be assumed to have perished. The stretching process is not new. I have no note of the source of the following quotation, but it dates from 1799:

Facts teach us, that *liberté* signifies the most horrible tyranny, silencing all law, and violating all property; that *égalité* signifies murdering sovereigns and the higher classes, and putting over the people men the most low, ignorant, and wicked, invested with power to insult, enslave, and drive them in flocks to be slaughtered, and placing them at a greater distance than there existed before between them and their superiors by birth and education. *Fraternité*, in France, signifies being a Frenchman; applied to other nations, it signifies, forcing on them a government, plundering their property, and taking their wives and daughters. *Philanthropie* is professing a general love to all mankind, and practising cruelty to every individual. *Philosophie* signifies the commission of every crime without remorse; the extinction of every sentiment religious or moral, of every generous and social feeling; the dissolution of every tie of kindred and affection; the annihilation of every quality which ornaments and distinguishes the gentleman, the scholar, and the man of taste; the banishment of chastity, modesty, sensibility, and decorum from the female sex.

Who, giving a moment's thought to what has been done in our own time in the name of 'democracy', could possibly support it or give it two cheers? E. M. Forster could. He found it less hateful than other contemporary forms of government; he credited it with the assumption that the individual is important, and that it takes all sorts to make a civilization; he found that it allows criticism, and some degree of liberty to the creative. But order, for him (it later appeared), was 'something evolved from within, not something imposed from without'. For him, yes, because he is an artist; but unfortunately what is called democracy tends more and more, like any other form of government, to impose what it calls order upon as many of the people as possible, as rigidly as possible, from without. It is a mark of E. M. Forster's energy and honesty that, instead of assuming an air of superiority and roosting more or less contentedly in the snug debris of liberalism, he has constantly tried to adjust himself to the phrases of the revolution through which he has lived, without deserting what he has believed to be true, and without relaxing that 'moral intelligence', without lowering that 'shield of Achilles'.

It is a commonplace that the artist, especially since the Romantic movement, has tended to be a solitary, an independent, an anarchist, or even a misanthrope. But the notion has become more and more accepted that it is now not only the artist's duty but his function to commit himself to public affairs. In the Canning Place days I should have been even less interested than I am now in theorizing on such a topic: but I do know that one of my main reasons for admiring E. M. Forster was that moral intelligence of the artist with which he had observed, felt, imagined, and embodied the relations between races in India. From the nature of my earliest life, I had been driven to observe inter-racial contacts and social incompatibilities, and, as I said in the preface to *Four Countries*, most of my own fiction reflects the age 'by isolating some crisis caused by a change of environment or by the sudden and sometimes startling confrontation of members of different races and classes'. It was, therefore, natural that I took special pleasure in being with him. Many of my closest friends have been unconformables, and of all my unconformable friends he has had, I think, the clearest, subtlest, deepest mind, the most generous understanding, and the most fruitfully revolutionary influence.

8

The Summer Robe

ANTHONY BUTTS's path and mine diverged, but our friendship lasted until his death, which occurred in 1941. After we gave up the house in Canning Place I removed to the two top floors of a house in that region near The Boltons which is not quite of Kensington, turns its back to Earl's Court, holds aloof from Chelsea, and a hundred years ago was called New Brompton. The road was quiet and had a neutral atmosphere that I found congenial.

When I went to the post office I used sometimes to encounter a lady of the upper middle class with whom I had a nodding acquaintance. She was evidently advanced in her views, because she hung about offering copies of the *Daily Worker* for sale. A little earlier, she would have been a suffragette; a little later, an existentialist. To advertise what she was selling, she had a newsbill fastened near her navel with a safety pin. The first time I saw her there, she was about to proffer a copy of the paper when the newsbill came adrift and slid to the ground. 'I'm afraid you've lost your poster,' I said, much as one might say, 'Excuse my saying so, but your slip is showing.' And I picked it up for her. By some fatality, certainly not by design, this doctrinaire apron collapsed twice more at the very moment when I happened to be the person nearest to her. The third time, while she thanked me almost effusively and showed what light novelists used to call 'a pretty confusion', I had to pin the thing to her jumper because neither of her hands was free. And talking of hands, I think it may have been on that very day that the newsbill carried the slogan *Hands off China*! I believe these brief encounters were the nearest I ever came to Communism, which some English writers of my generation appeared to regard as hopefully as a new star in the east.

It is part of the intention of this book to sketch or suggest its author's relationship to a few of the persons he has admired and places he has known—to a few, not to all. If, in doing so, he has so far happened to give any impression of detachment, of equanimity, or even of urbanity, let these things be attributed to a retrospective mood, not to a pose. If he has said little or nothing about being lonely, or needy, or downcast, or anxious, that is not because he was a stranger to any of those conditions. He knows what it is to be ill, to be in pain, to be disappointed, to be misunderstood, to be cheated, to be insulted, to be frustrated: we live in a world where such things occur. But he has no inclination to compile a hard-luck story; and if he does not dwell upon actions of his own that were foolish and others of which he is ashamed, that is because his way of writing memoirs is not to turn them into a public confessional or a parade of vain regrets.

To look back is all very well, to select, to weigh, and to measure, but there was plenty of folly in my life in the Thirties. There were things I wanted to find out, and I found them out. If I were to survive into old age and retain my faculties, and feel inclined to contemplate 'the ash of all I burned' when young (the phrase is Wilfred Owen's), I should hope not to moisten it with useless tears but to recall happily the fires of which it is the residue. I wore what Jeremy Taylor called 'the light and phantastic summer robe of lust'. Much time and energy were used up by me in the pursuit of chimeras—and exceedingly magnetic some of them were. Obsessively, and sometimes recklessly, I pursued illusions—and

sometimes caught them: sometimes it was bitter to lose them, and
sometimes it was a relief. I asked more of life than it could reason-
ably have been expected to give; but I was not guided by reason.
In a letter I wrote to my parents at this time I find:

> By the way, Joe says he has never seen anyone so up and down
> as I am—so choppiness is evidently hereditary. He says he
> doesn't know how I can write, because I'm 'always in an
> emotional storm.'

Joe was J. R. Ackerley. He was then living in a cottage of character wedged in between the Mall and the river at Hammersmith.
I had first seen him at Savoy Hill in the summer of 1929, in
connection with some broadcast. There was a heatwave, and he
looked so cool and self-possessed in his white silk shirt that I was
a little frightened of him. Elegant to the point of dandyism, and
fine-featured, he had (like Herbert Read) the gentleness of manner
that sometimes goes with strong convictions, independence, and
pugnacity. The mixture of directness and vagueness in his manner
made me nervous of being a bore.

By the time I was living in New Brompton I had begun to know
him better. His book *Hindoo Holiday* was and is generally admired.
To me it had a special appeal. Together with *A Passage to India* it
seemed truthful in a new way, and a new approach to Asians on
the part of an Englishman. I was magnetized by its freedom from
preconceived notions, its unwincing directness, and its surgeon-
like delicacy. It was delicate, but it probed. Again, like the work of
E. M. Forster, it suggested a character in some ways formidable.
Then there was his play *The Prisoners of War*, an early and idio-
syncratic work in the huge literature of imprisonment which this
age of persecution and punishment has produced. How fortunate
I was that so humane a heart should put up with my vacillations of

mood, and that such an unsullied eye and understanding should perceive and not condemn my pursuit of chimeras! His patience gave me shelter in my then unceasing 'emotional storm'.

Chekhov says that love is 'either the shrinking remnant of something which once was enormous; or else it is a part of something which will grow in the future into something enormous. But in the present it does not satisfy. It gives much less than one expects.' It is because love is never wholly satisfying that a man without weighty ambitions or responsibilities can so easily make a cult of sex, the more because of those moments when love seems to attain perfection, as if disclosing what it once was or some day may be. Such moments may be but are not necessarily those of coition, or of physical contact or mere proximity, and they seem closely related to those other moments of religious or artistic experience when an extraordinary equipoise or harmony is reached and sometimes sustained, when it seems as if the world were properly, or ideally, organized after all; or as if the sky itself had suddenly opened, and the ear had caught hitherto unimagined harmonies. A line of poetry can open the sky, or a flourish of Handel's, a serenade with fiddles and flutes in the dead of night on a Greek island, a solitary prayer, or, if one is attuned to it, anything in nature, any work of art. All the world is open to the senses, and more than the world to that extra sense that transcends them.

To intervals of solitude I was accustomed but not always reconciled. If you never find yourself alone, said Gide, you will never find yourself at all. But as soon as you *have* found yourself, he might have added, it is time to hurry back to others. If you overhear solitaries talking to themselves, you seldom find them saying anything worth hearing. There is often a tone of complaint in their utterances. They rely too much upon themselves in their judgment of others, and because the world seems to have abandoned them, their judgment of the world is unfavourable.

In the late Thirties, on fine afternoons, there was a lady who used to sit on a particular seat on the front at Brighton, facing the sea and the strolling promenaders. Even when other persons were sitting beside her, she was conspicuously alone. In her late fifties or early sixties, she was respectably (as they say) but not fashionably dressed, and rigidly corseted in the Edwardian style. On her head she always wore the same hat, a toque trimmed in front with a pair of rampant white wings. Pointing skyward, north-west and north-east, they were faintly yellowed with age and exposure, and not very securely fastened; they wobbled slightly.

'Men!' I was startled to hear her exclaim gruffly the first time I saw her. I was passing by, but slowed down, leant on the railing within earshot, and looked intently out to sea for the ship I was not expecting. '*Men!*' she cried. 'I hate them all!' A pause. Then, with withering contempt: '*Husband*! He *called* himself a husband! The dirty, lowdown, sneaking, deceitful *rotter!*' Then a mumbling, then crescendo: 'Men! *So-called* men! *Rotters*, that's what they are! *Rotters!*'

I moved on. I often saw and heard her again. One day I heard her say, with an ineffable disgust that might have given hints to Mrs Siddons, 'Sold my furniture!' Other people constantly saw and heard her too. In the tolerant way of the English they would nudge one another, give her a glance, and stroll uneasily on, as if ignoring an almost indecent exposure. Children, or coarse oldish women, would sometimes stare and giggle; men, feeling stigmatized, would slink past or, indifferent, stride past.

On and on went the tirade, and she nodded her head vigorously. She was like an actress putting herself wholly into her part. But it seemed a part in a morality play. Perhaps she represented Death itself. The wings in her hat looked steely in certain lights, they were blade-like, a pair of abhorred shears. Would they suddenly, softly, irrevocably close? Or would a more than usually energetic nod one day unhinge them, making the blades fall uselessly apart? If that happened, she would cease to protest; she would collapse like a puppet; she would at last surrender; with the falling apart of those exalted emblems of her will and personality, both would disintegrate; arthritis, suddenly tightening its screws, would keep her indoors for the rest of her time, and never again would she be able to harangue the gusty breezes bustling up the Channel from the Atlantic, the expressionless southern sky, or the promenaders pretending that she could be neither seen nor heard.

Then one day, just as I was going past, she accidentally dropped her tall, thin umbrella. I picked it up and as I handed it to her I smiled. She beamed as if electrified.

'Oh, thank you! Thank you so much! How very kind of you!'

Gracious, radiant, benevolent! The poor soul was suffering from something quite different from the pleasure of solitude, she was suffering from the disease of loneliness. Can it have been that all she wanted was a male in her life, any male not a 'rotter', a male who, instead of making away with her furniture, would occasionally bring her a cup of early morning tea, tell her she needed a new hat (and how she needed it!), notice it when she had bought it, and take her out to the pictures, or to church, or to inhale the sea air? But the likelihood of such a male presenting himself seemed fanciful.

Solitude is not the same thing as loneliness. No man could have seemed more sociable, less solitary, than Laurence Oliphant, that strange Victorian full of the energy and enterprise so characteristic of his time: but he was isolated, madly isolated. His biographer, Mr Philip Henderson, records his having written:

> The world, with its bloody wars, its political intrigues, its social evils, its religious cant, its financial frauds, and its glaring anomalies, assumed in my eyes more and more the aspect of a gigantic lunatic asylum.*

There is an Oliphant in all of us, and a century later any of us could say the same: but how dangerous to say it! To feel wise alone is to feel oneself superior to the rest of mankind: one thinks the world mad when one is mad oneself. And that is the time when people are tempted to rely upon and submit to the discipline of some system claiming absolute authority, like Roman Catholicism or Marxism. To crave for absolute authority is a form of infantilism, and no system, whatever its claims, possesses or can maintain absolute authority. Yet if one is left to one's resources they will sooner or later be found inadequate.

It is the fate of more people, it appears, in the twentieth century than in previous times to move about, to live in exile, and to share the material advantages of some community with which they have little in common and little or no sense of community—particularly in urban or suburban surroundings. Persons with no strong religious or political adhesions, without assessable property, or children, or even a settled family life, and either self-employed, casually employed, or unemployed, may find themselves living in a state of fatalistic suspense that cannot be called good. Such was the condition of many people in England between the Wars, and such, in the Thirties, was mine. Perhaps if I had understood it more clearly, I could have snapped out of it; perhaps not.

* *The Life of Laurence Oliphant*, by Philip Henderson. Hale, 1956.

The Summer Robe

'There can clearly be now no question of our meeting in Munich', I find in a letter to my parents written in 1933, about a plan for one of our meetings abroad. We were already confronted with what David Gascoyne has called those 'years like a prison-wall', and perhaps no English poet has commemorated more exactly that poisoned atmosphere of the ineluctable:

> ... night by night the same
> Weary anabasis
> Between two wars, towards
> The Future's huge abyss.

Some people valiantly tried to prevent what could not be prevented, some to cure what was incurable. The majority, as usual, were blindly indifferent; without knowing it, they were afflicted with moral drought, with a partial eclipse of the will. Without understanding it, I was in the grip of the same affliction. Now that I think I understand it, I do not see how I could have been in any other condition. At the risk of boring the reader, I must say a little about the more personal reasons for my having succumbed to it. Who knows? A chance word may help somebody somewhere to avoid something of the same sort.

Looking back from a distance, I see that the First World War, at the beginning of which I was still a child, produced a deep trauma in me. What! Have I the face to say that, of a war in which millions were killed? I have. Is it not indecent to draw attention to private woes in a time of general calamity? It may be, but I have had to live with the consequences of both. I had been brought up in atmospheres where it was generally accepted without question that one belonged to a race that enjoyed, as if by Divine right, a moral and material superiority which gave it the leadership of the world. Under the pax Britannica the world would go radiantly forward under the guidance and dominance of Englishmen imbued in church from an early age with a sense of sin, on the cricket field with a mystically combined sense of fair play and the team spirit, and, from reading Kipling, with a sense of their own high destiny. Pervading everything was an ideal, seldom explicit, of gentlemanliness, which included such things as not boasting, not hurting other people's feelings, never letting others feel inferior, being kind to the weak, the poor, and the old, and regarding cruelty and falsehood as the greatest of evils.

In a disposition naturally critical it was natural that scepticism should put out early shoots. One does not have to be very old to see that not everybody practises what he preaches. At a very early age I could not help having difficulty in taking cricket seriously. What was all the fuss about? Like other games it needed practice and skill, but it seemed slow, and an elaborate way of wasting time in fine weather, when one might be doing much more enjoyable things, or doing nothing in particular. The tedium of spoken or written discussion of cricket scores or the form of its players seems to me as colossal as the fond freemasonry of the game's addicts seems incomprehensible: some of my best friends are batty about cricket, but we never meet at Lord's or crouch together to attend to what the wireless calls 'a ball by ball commentary'.

I suppose it was the smug assumption that cricket playing was a sign of racial superiority that helped to put me against it. The same grown-ups who treated cricket almost as a religious exercise, and religion as if it were a form of cricket, spoke of Kipling's works or read them aloud as if they were the Gospel itself. Christopher Isherwood has told how they were read aloud on Sunday afternoons at his preparatory school, almost as if part of the curriculum, and how the things Kipling approved of seemed to him aspects of an Enemy he knew he would have to fight for the rest of his life. I understand this perfectly, but it does not wholly blind me, any more than it has blinded him, to the great gifts of the man who could write a line like

> I have paid my price to live with myself
> on the terms that I willed.

I could not know that Henry James, in a letter written several years before I was born, had said of Kipling, 'Almost nothing civilized save steam and patriotism — and the latter only in verse, where I *hate* it so, mixed up with God and goodness. . . .' Definitions of God and goodness had not been kept from me, but I could not reconcile them with jingoism or with war, though my grandfather was a professional soldier and so were two of his sons, the third being an amateur. At a very early age I was shown a portrait of an uncle. 'That is poor Uncle Durham,' said my mother, 'who was killed in the war.' I said 'Why?' and am still waiting for an answer: he was killed in the Boer War.

No child of my generation of even minimal intelligence or sensibility could have remained untroubled by what went on in France from 1914 onwards. What had it to do with peace, or loving one's neighbour, or with forgiveness of one's enemies? Were torpedoes, tanks, and poison gas linked in some way with fair play and not hurting other people's feelings? 'Thou shalt do no murder', said the commandment. But what was being done in France? Was not Cain killing Abel over and over again? For those of my generation in whom these questions had laid their eggs, the temperature of the Twenties could only promote a hatching. I could remember an experienced soldier of the regular Army, something of an authority on the theory as well as the practice of warfare, saying in August, 1914, 'It'll all be over by

Christmas.' I had known all the wishful cant about Tommy Atkins, and the Russian steam roller, and the war to end war, and making the world safe for democracy. How could we look forward with hope, with another and probably far more destructive World War in prospect? Whom and what were we to trust in? Military judgment, political wisdom, the ill-defined 'man in the street'? How could war promote peace?

At this point it seems right to summon up poor Uncle Durham. He was poor only in the sense that it was thought a pity he had been killed in the prime of life. The son of a kindly and fairly rich father, of decent birth and conventional upbringing, at ease in any society he might find himself in, established in the military profession, a healthy extravert, good-looking, good-humoured, athletic, fond of women and attractive to them, he was a fortunate son of a civilization apparently at its climax.

'What's all this rot,' I seem to hear him say, 'about disillusionment, and cricket, and Kipling? You're alive, aren't you, and free? If other men hadn't given up their freedom and allowed themselves to be deprived of their lives, you mightn't be either alive or free . . . Kipling? Not much time for reading, myself. Or inclination. But they say he's good . . . I played cricket for Cheltenham, and enjoyed it.' (At this point he gives particulars of an innings in some match.) 'When my regiment was sent to South Africa, I naturally went with it. I happened to stop a Boer bullet, and that's all. Bad luck, perhaps, but I didn't have a bad life; I enjoyed almost every moment of it.'

'If I may say so,' I reply, 'you were shoved into the Army because your father thought it the best place for you. You were a good soldier, you did your duty, you were killed in action, you were missed, and for a time you were grieved for. An inscribed stone was put up over your corpse. . . . But there is another side to all this. You did what you were told, because your profession demanded obedience. But whom were you obeying? You probably had no doubts of the wisdom of those who had made British troops invade so distant a country. But their wisdom and their morality were questioned by many of your own contemporaries, who thought that war unnecessary, unwise, and unprincipled.'

'Ugh!' he replies. 'Pro-Boers!'

'What good do you suppose that war did? Do you think it made England loved? Do you know the Boers call it the Second War of Independence? Did you think you were helping to make South Africa a permanent colony? Today, in all but name, it's a Boer republic . . . In *your* time you were so confident. This is *my* century, and we're not so cocky and light-hearted as you were. Our doubts are precious to us. Without them all that is still left of what you imagined you fought for will be destroyed, and mankind itself may come to an end.'

'But you've got to believe in *something*,' he says gently. He wrinkles his forehead. He is puzzled and yet not hostile: he sees that I seem to mean what I say. 'If you give in to doubt, surely you won't want to do anything at all.'

It would be difficult to explain to him that at an age when he was bursting with energy and hope at Sandhurst, I had been isolated in the altogether remote and alien atmosphere of Tokyo, and much influenced by the outlook of my Japanese friends and coevals there. Smiling sadly, I shake his cold hand, and let him fade back into the hero's grave at Nooitgedacht . . .

The importance of maintaining my own being did not seem to me, I dare say, any greater than it had to poor Uncle Durham, or the importance of maintaining European civilization any less. But I believed that if it was to be done with weapons, the weapons most immediately appropriate were doubt and disgust. If these machetes, I felt, were in more general and strenuous use, ways out of the encroaching jungle might be steadily hacked: but time was short, and the more nearly a State became totalitarian, the stricter the taboo upon their use, and the rarer the skill and courage to use them.

I was not without beliefs. I believed in art and literature and the devotion of those who produce them—though what I meant by art and literature was far from the cheap or precious meanings with which those words are sometimes invested. I loved individuals. I saw this belief and this love, which together had led me to live as I was living, conjoined as one creative function, outside which I had no ambition. I do not say my way of living was virtuous, or the best possible for my purpose, but the increasing tension and despair of the world's prospects did not leave the spirit free or the judgment calm. To be deficient in hope is unchristian. I was deficient in hope, and a lapsed Christian.

9

Not Alone in London

FROM New Brompton I had removed to a quiet ground floor
flat in Maida Vale. On one side was a house with a plaque
to commemorate Sir John Tenniel. On the other gleamed the
leafy Regent's Canal, where a grimmer fantasy than his seemed to
be at work one morning when a casual angler mistook for a 'bite'
the waterlogged body of an unwanted infant.

To judge from the reactions of certain ageing types to any
mention of Maida Vale, the quarter was thought louche. It had
the reputation of having abounded in the nesting places of kept
women, generally of a lower status than those who had been set
up earlier in the pretty villas of St John's Wood. By my time
economic and social changes had made it more conspicuously a
quarter of unkept women—unkept, but not unkempt. Even before lighting-up time, prinked-up figures swathed in silver fox
capes and hoisted on high-heeled shoes were to be seen stationed
all along the pavements, at regular intervals like lamp posts. So
clearly demarcated were their spheres of influence that one could
hardly help knowing one's own strumpet. The occupational
hazards of scandal and crime were such that the local newsagent,
if asked for the national Sunday newspaper most given to re-
porting such things, used to say sardonically, 'You mean the
Maida Vale Gazette.' All the same, the quarter was largely what
used to be called respectable. There were houses not yet divided
into flats, inherited and still occupied by retired lawyers or old

rentier spinsters, sub-Forsytes stuck fast, it appeared, in a habit of life as dull, fusty, and outmoded as what could be seen of their heavy furniture or as the blackish laurels in their gardens. The gaslight and gloom, the silent back streets with noisy, baroque public houses at each end, and the heaviness of the architecture all helped to maintain the late Victorian atmosphere, which for me had strangeness and a kind of glamour.

There was one place in London where it was possible to indulge less vaguely my taste (which was not fashionable but personal) for the energy, oddity, and variety of England in the nineteenth century. That was the Caledonian Market. In the pale light of some Friday morning in autumn that great open space and its adjacent buildings, with its groups and strolling couples and absence of motor traffic had the very tints and ambience of a scene in a Victorian lithograph, and there, spread out at one's feet, were long, long avenues of treasures and treasurable trash. It is perhaps as well that I lacked the cravings, the means, the leisure, and the storage space of a collector, otherwise I could easily have accumulated a whole museum. Down those avenues I loitered, looking perhaps like the last of the flâneurs, but animated in fact by an almost suffocating and quite unrational excitement: it was the appetite—one of the appetites—of a poet. And this appetite was fed, but never appeased, by the pleasure of seeing and touching sauceboats and sovereign purses, fans and cigar cases; a Gothic chair, or an old, well made chest of smoothly sliding drawers; a banner-like firescreen, worked in turquoise and white beads with a flying angel; a cross set with agates, or a pair of coral earrings carved in the shape of a hand holding a Grecian urn; a discarded group photograph of a family, showing a virgin in a bustle, a little aloof from the rest under an ivied rustic arch, her eyes big with frozen hope; or a stereoscopic view of Leamington in the eighteen-seventies with a stationary cab immobilized and almost, but not quite, immortalized by the camera. To enjoy a sense of the essence of the vanished age from which I had derived and in the last phase of which I had come to consciousness—I suppose this might be written off as escapism or a psychological culpable re-version to something or other. I do not see it like that. I was too much amused by the ingenuities of craftsmanship and the aberrations of taste, and too touched all the time by a peculiar sense of the transitoriness of life. I have always been a keen escapist from the banal and the fashionable, and enjoy ignoring the dogmatic assertions of half-baked doctrinaires and being left free to follow up clues to social history. And, by the way, not everything at the Market was Victorian; it was just the place to pick up cheaply a handsome pair of curtains, a set of bookshelves, or other useful furniture.

Under my nose—and indeed above it, on the upper floors—and all around were change, decay, and new life. In a house not far away lived a then well-known film star, who was to be seen stalking about now and then with a long upper lip, a walking stick, and a self-consciously proprietorial air. The fact that he was chosen to impersonate legendary nineteenth-century characters, the Duke of Wellington probably, Disraeli certainly, and I dare say Gladstone as well, was in itself a measure of the gulf that already separated us from their time. It was the fictionist rather than the poet in me who took a keen interest in the social revolution going on all round me, and I regarded with the utmost curiosity the types and individuals of everyday life in this and other parts of London.

Not all the living that went on in Maida Vale was loose, probably only a very small proportion of it. There were plenty of inconspicuous and thrifty couples, and single persons, of office-

going or shop-owning habit; and there were marginal or unaccountable figures, seedy or showy, about whose invisible means
of subsistence it was tempting to speculate and instructive to learn.
The landlady of that house over there let out her rooms to hopeful
students of drama and ballet. Clearly a dog addict, she could be
seen towing a wan Bedlington to the greengrocer's. 'Isn't he a
lamb?' she was heard to say—and he almost was. Another of her
sayings was addressed to a young girl who asked if she might receive a male visitor in her room. 'I don't care what you do in your
room,' said the landlady, 'so long as you don't set it on fire.' She
was said to be a failed contralto, and I should like to have a tape
recording of her making that pronouncement. That man with the
military air of twenty years earlier was said to be a cashiered ex-
subaltern basking in the false afterglow of a manufactured past. He
had been seen at Somerset House, and was rumoured to get a
living by manufacturing other pasts, in the shape of pedigrees, for
the socially aspiring descendants of emigrants overseas. That poor
wight with a stoop who goes often to the pillar box might perhaps be doing precarious hackwork as a translator; he looks as if
he were maintaining an invalid wife who no longer gets com-
missions for those sugary miniatures of children she used to do.

There had always been a cultural element in these parts, from
the days when Browning and Edmund Gosse had lived in houses
overlooking the canal basin, which the author of *Sinister Street* was
said to have overlooked rather later. And now among my notable
neighbours were Joe Ackerley, Stephen Spender, and Air-
Commodore (retired) L. E. O. Charlton. A joke was current
about our constituting a 'Maida Vale Group', but we were all too
independent, too obviously barking (or refraining from barking)
up different trees, or too deficient in team spirit, even to want, let
alone attempt, to form anything like a group. Stephen Spender,

with his mingled air of surprise, self-confidence, and ruddy health, was by now turning his attention ever more closely to European continental politics: he was not at all of the kind of solitary, introverted, doomed poets of the Romantic tradition, but an example of a twentieth-century kind that feel it necessary to be if not in the news at least not behind the times.

General Charlton (as he was usually called) I had first met at one of T. S. Eliot's *Criterion* parties. The author of an autobiography written in the third person, he had in fact been a general in the Army before the first World War. He had served with dash and bravery in the Boer War, had served in West Africa, and had so distinguished himself in the Royal Flying Corps that he was later believed to be all set to rise to a great altitude in the Royal Air Force. Posted to Iraq in 1923 as chief of staff at R.A.F. headquarters, he found that on grounds of conscience he could not support what he regarded as a policy of indiscriminate bombing of unarmed villagers, including women and children. He made it known that he considered it 'a species of oppression which tended to render infamous the British name for fair dealing throughout the world'. He accordingly asked to be relieved of his duties, deliberately relinquishing his professional advancement, and before long had retired into private life. Independent, high-spirited, and well-bred as a racehorse, this honourable man came of an ancient Northumbrian Roman Catholic family, the Charltons of Hesleyside. The *Memoirs of a Northumbrian Lady* which he later edited and published are of uncommon historical, social, and regional interest. From Maida Vale he afterwards migrated to Dover.

Joe Ackerley had, I think, already been promoted literary editor of the *Listener*, a post in which his taste and conscientiousness were to be brought to bear for many years. I had now become

At Home

familiar with his unique personality. Brushing aside what seemed to him inessentials, going straight to what seemed to him the point of any subject or situation, impelled by a logic of his own, unhindered by ordinary usage, convention, or prejudice, rendered acute by the workings of an inquiring, literal, totally uninventive yet artistically selective mind, and independent by unworldliness and a kind of innocence, he made an impression of troubled candour and rare purity—troubled, because his face often wore a look of anxiety. When interested, his powers of concentration were those of a burning glass, but his trains of thought, as obstinate and as surefooted as mules, seemed often to lead him far from the place where he was and the person or persons he was with—over almost inaccessible paths, one imagined, with an abyss on one side and the threat of a landslide on the other. His introspective processes of inquiry, analysis, judgment, and speculation often gave him an abstracted air.

With all the detachment of a somnambulist he once went into a teashop at Shepherd's Bush to drink tea. He sat down at a table for two. The chair opposite his was already occupied by an elderly woman. If his attention had been caught by her he would at once have registered every detail of her appearance and bearing. Like Gogol, he might have said 'Je ne parvenais à déviner la nature d'un homme que lorsque je voyais clairement les moindres détails de son extérieur.' But his thoughts were far away, and quite without knowing it he was gazing at her as intently as if she were an aircraft pin-pointed high up in a cloudless sky.

'Oh!' she cried, under the gimlet of his scrutiny, 'what piercing eyes!'

Slowly returning to consciousness, he said with the utmost surprise, after looking round over his shoulder: 'Is it possible that you mean me?'

Not Alone in London

'Yes, I do,' she said. 'I think you must be a customs officer.'

'Then,' he said, with his usual quick-wittedness and charming smile, 'I can only ask if you have anything to declare.'

It was the valuable policy of the *Listener* to pay much attention to the art of painting. He was a constant visitor therefore to new exhibitions and became a discriminating appreciator not only of pictures but of art critics. Before lunching together one day, probably at the Café Royal, we looked in at Burlington House for a preview of one of the great special exhibitions, which had just been hung. As the galleries were almost empty we could see the pictures without being distracted by the pleasure of meeting friends or the bother of being obstructed by a crowd. But he seemed to have something on his mind. He was carrying under his arm not a parcel but a round object as big as a croquet ball and untidily wrapped in some loose and crumpled sheets of the *Daily Mirror*. I knew what it was, because I had asked him: it was a cauliflower he had bought on his way. He had said that he wasn't altogether happy about it. He suspected that it wasn't quite fresh. As happens with the Brassicae in such a condition, it was making its presence perceptible—or he thought it was. Telegraph wires of anxiety appeared on his forehead, and it was evident that the place where he had bought the vegetable, the bona fides and manner of its vendor, its destiny, the possibility that his suspicion was after all unfounded, etc., were all engaging his attention to the exclusion of the successive masterpieces upon which his eyes were turned, as if searching for contraband or, Roger Fry-like, for evidence of a false attribution.

As we moved into one of the larger galleries, a distant and solitary figure, dressed (as novelists say) 'immaculately' and in the style of a banker or diplomatist, was to be seen gazing at a picture.

'Ah!' Joe Ackerley exclaimed, and hurried forward. It was a cry of recognition: the solitary figure was the Director-General of the British Broadcasting Corporation. This important person, after acknowledging our presence with a restrained greeting, looked with unconcealed distaste at the untidy sheets of the popular newspaper so ill wrapped round what might have been something inappropriate, unclean, or even sinister.

'Do you know anything about cauliflowers?' he was charmingly asked without preliminaries. 'The reason I ask is—'

And a moment later the important man was to be seen half unbending to pretend to catch whatever effluvium might be rising from the proffered object, now half unveiled. The naturalness of this proceeding reflected credit on both, but the third person present found it, in those surroundings, characteristic and exquisitely incongruous.

A migrant life has its advantages, but among the things against it are that it tends to disrupt some personal relationships—those, for instance, of a domestic kind. Both my parents, who, as I have indicated elsewhere, led nomadic lives, used to win the hearts of their servants, white or black, not by spoiling them but by treating them in the traditional old English way as persons in their own right. It was taken for granted that obligations were mutual. A servant did work and was paid for it, but it was the employer's function to help and protect the servant, in health or sickness, in happiness or trouble. Each did his best to promote the well-being of the other. From my earliest days in Edwardian England and South Africa I had seen admirable examples of the master-and-servant relationship, beautiful when it brings out the best in the nature of each and creates an equilibrium of trust, security, and mutual aid. But even at an early age I had seen tears running down a good black face and the sight of them causing tears to blur the eyes of my mother at one of those all too frequent moments of necessary parting. In my own life, too, besides the pangs of parting from persons more intimately beloved, I had felt the sadness of losing the services of others who had looked after one's daily needs, faithfully and without complaint. And so it was in London.

At New Brompton, as at Canning Place, I had had the help of what is called a daily woman. She was not in the least like the type of charwoman so standardized by cheap plays and radio plays that charwomen now try and live up to the conventional level of big breasted, never downhearted, wisecracking, synthetic Cockney trollophood. No, Mrs Lydamore was small, neat, delicate. She had to be helped to lift heavy weights. She was neither shabby nor genteel, but clean as a cat, was never heard to complain or say an unkind word, and was sustained in her widowhood by one idea — the well-being of her young and only son in Canada — and by one prospect, that of seeing him again. In Maida Vale, to which it was not possible to bring Mrs Lydamore, I took on, during my first sojourn there, a daily man called Rainbird. He, too, I am glad to say, conformed to no type. Punctual, sober, deft, clean, tolerant, and a good cook, he was a married man, but spent all his spare time, when the weather allowed, flying kites which he had made himself. I do not understand well the attractions of this obsession, which I had also noticed in Japan, but I suppose it gives a feeling of solitariness, of power, of freedom, tranquillity, and soaring exaltation which may be of healing value to the bruised and constricted spirit of an urban man.

I was to return to Maida Vale about 'the time of Munich', to unusually large rooms in Randolph Crescent, which I only left after they had been damaged by bombing and looted. Between what I may call my first and second Maida Vale periods I was absent from London. At the beginning of the second I interviewed a number of prospective daily men, hoping for another Rainbird. I was impressed by their individuality. One was too emotional and perhaps hoped to be more than a servant. Another would do anything but cook. A third seemed to have been born in a tiny green baize apron; his pride and joy, he explained, was to clean silver in all his waking hours. His feeling for silver seemed as instinctive as that of some men for horses or pigeons and my few spoons would soon have built up in him a terrible frustration. For a moment I almost wished my parents had not got rid of some of those inherited objects, silver candelabra, or the soup tureen which had been used by one of my forefathers when Lord Mayor of London in the seventeen-eighties. Instead I engaged Utting.

At an early age Utting had been injured in the First World War. A smallish, stocky, compact man with a veiny complexion and small eyes, he was a most helpful and unfussy maintainer of a simple domestic rhythm. We never had more than brief colloquy, but when Utting did speak I had the impression that his view of the universe and of the immediate foreground was very much his own. He lodged in or near Lisson Grove, in Marylebone, and one day seemed anxious to tell me about something that had gone wrong at his lodgings. I listened attentively.

'It's my landlord,' he said.

'Oh, yes.'

'He's troubled with boils on the neck. And his wife, she's got boils on her feet.'

'What a nuisance,' I said. 'Perhaps they're both a bit run down.'

'No, it's not that. He says it's because they were both born in October.'

'Libra, or Scorpio?'

'Pardon?'

Not Alone in London

'Oh, nothing,' I said.

'But she won't have it,' said Utting. 'She will have it that it's the water.'

'The water?' I echoed.

'It's not that,' he said. 'I know what it is. It's the smell from the animals.'

'The animals?' I seemed cast for the part of Echo. 'Why, Utting? Do they keep a lot of pets?'

'No, no, it's not that. It's the Zoo.'

His belief was that the wind, when it blew from the direction of the Zoo, more than a mile away on the far side of the Regent's Park, brought with it a contagion which caused boils. This did not seem scientific, but rather the theory of a man conscious of the pressure of strange natural forces around and within us. It was not strange to me; it was the sort of belief one might have found in Zululand, but I should not have expected to find it in London.

I found many unexpected things in London. It should not be thought that I was so disengaged from the life of the time that I had retreated into a Victorian dream world. Not at all. In the mid-Thirties I brought out a novel, *The Invaders*, which was a fruit of curiosity about the answers to such questions as what might happen to a girl from the country who came up to London on her own to make her living and drifted into different employments, and to a boy who came to London and joined the Army, and how the lives of such 'invaders' might interact with the lives of persons of a different class or different racial origin. As in *The Case is Altered*, I was concerned with what happened to a variety of persons brought together in London by changing social conditions, and with their feelings. Some people thought it the best of the four novels I had written, some did not. I was confident that I had written a book that was not superficial, and I knew it was full of truth about people and what happened to them; it was presented, I hoped, with a certain freshness. The inside view of military life in London in peacetime caused the leading non-commissioned officer of a well-known regiment to place a copy of the book before the colonel commanding it: he deferentially suggested that it would help that officer to understand better the lives and conditions of the men under his command. The book was also thought well of by those of my friends who had experience of social work and a better idea of the gulf that separated South Kensington from the purlieus of the Edgware Road than had certain literary intellectuals of the know-all type.

It is the business of the novelist not so much to see life as to see it from the point of view of others — one might say of *any* others, so far as that is possible. In England this often meant learning to see members of one class from the point of view of another. A good friend of mine was Jack Carey, a roadworker, or navvy, of about my own age. He was not a Londoner, and it was interesting to see the people of London through his eyes, and to notice how the little things that happened to him and his mates in the course of their work sometimes indicated social change — or no change. He had no political views and, being of an independent nature, no class consciousness.

He found that the public were mostly ill-mannered and inconsiderate; that motorists were the most selfish and insolent people, and that the worst of them were taxi drivers or women. It was nothing unusual for a motorist to knock down the roadmen's poles and trestles and drive on without apology. Twice my friend had himself been knocked down by impatient motorists. Once when he and his party were repairing a pavement (which he called a 'footway') in Mayfair a tall military-looking man came out of a house and said:

Not Alone in London

'What's all this mess?'

'It's all right, Captain,' said one of the roadmen civilly, 'we'll soon be finished.'

'Colonel to you!' the man bellowed.

'Oh yes?' said my friend quietly. 'We're not living in those times now.'

The man glared and snorted, got into his car, and slammed the door in a rage.

Only once in my friend's experience had a rich person shown any consideration: that was when a lady sent her maid out to ask if the men would like some tea. One winter's day in a residential street it came on to rain very hard. The only shelter was in a doorway, and three of the roadmen stood in it. Suddenly the door opened and out came a woman who said, 'Get out of my doorway and don't make a mess with your muddy boots on my step!' They got off it, and one of the men said to her, 'You should have told us that in 1914, when we were looking after your interests. We had mud up to our necks then, and you called us heroes.' She had no answer, and banged the door in his face. He still had pieces of shrapnel in his body.

It is sometimes suggested that the writers of the Thirties were sentimental about what was still called the working class. What if they were? If Stephen Spender or George Orwell appeared to some to idealize or falsify the lives of persons of a lower level than that into which they had been born, perhaps that was necessary to their art and thought. Every considerable poet I have known has had some unusual concentration of interest, some fantasy or obsession or predilection which has been an essential motive force in his work. It may be a passion for a person, place, or thing; for a vice or a virtue; for Hindu mysticism, or neo-Gothic architecture; for the past or the future; for a civil war in Ireland or Spain; for a

At Home

dangerous political creed, a bad writer, or a deaf giantess; but whatever the fantasy, it has been more or less closely related to the significance of his own time or of the time that is to follow it. Every considerable poet opens a window, or even several windows, that nobody has ever opened, or even noticed, before: the greater the poet, the more wonderful and unfamiliar the view. But people don't take easily to unfamiliar views and visions; they like the shelter of cosy prejudices and accepted ideas.

It was not only radical politicians, social workers, or leftwing intellectuals who were conscious of the fate of the unemployed — of their numbers, and of the disintegrating effect of their condition upon personality as well as physique. Unemployment, as Archbishop Temple wrote later, is a 'corrosive poison', of which the worst effect is 'the moral disaster of not being wanted'. I found out by chance that my parents, whom I did not see very often, had been brooding over the problem. They had heard a bad account of South Shields, where they had never been in their lives, and they wrote to the Anglican incumbent there and asked him to put them in touch with a family suffering from that poison. This he did. My parents were no longer young. One was in the lifelong grip of a nervous illness, and the other in the tightening grip of a mortal illness; and through no wickedness of their own they were much less well off than they had been. Yet they were now prepared to do without things they would have liked and perhaps really needed, so that they could send from time to time small sums of money or material comforts to the family in South Shields. Scrupulously avoiding as far as possible the semblance of being charitable, they tried to vary the nature of their gifts and wrote letters inquiring about the welfare of various members of the family. They hoped to convey as unobtrusively as they could the sort of stimulus that may help those who have been feeling useless, unhopeful, undernourished, and unwanted to feel that they matter in their own right. The warm response of the widowed mother of the South Shields family was without false pride or servility: she showed the proper dignity of one who needs help, and is helped, and is pleased.

Anything my parents did for the betterment of that family was small and temporary. Born in mid-Victorian times, faithful but not fanatical Anglicans, they believed that it was an obligation to help those less fortunate than themselves, as a matter of ordinary humanity and Christian charity. Their forebears protected dependants and servants and poor neighbours; they themselves were displaced and migrant, and the world was their parish. It may have been too late to try and restore that sense of community which had been weakened or destroyed by industrialization, over-population, mobility, bureaucracy, and so on, but I felt nothing but respect for the thought and the action.

Extract from a letter to my parents:

I was present at the Means Test riot which you have no doubt read about, and got banged about by a mounted policeman, although I was merely looking on, not 'demonstrating'. I hear that the authorities had actually ordered the Guards to stand by. This seems rather a Czarist approach to the misery of the unemployed. Nearly forty policemen are said to have been injured. A shop was broken into by the crowd and looted. It had large notices advertising a 'Great Clearance Sale—Everything Must Go!' Everything did.

10

A Broken Chain

O F the pleasures of London none was sweeter than leaving it. After taking a train, being met by a car, and driven to some country house or house in the country, the visitor was immediately astonished, shocked, by the grassy silence. It fell on the ears like a blow: but the shock was therapeutic; the clean air was perceived by nose and throat and lungs, and by the skin itself, like a cool draught on a thirsty palate. A starving and parching time was suddenly known, by its temporary inter-ruption, to have existed. The sky and its phases were visible and open; the feet were conscious of pressing on the earth; and a moment had come to wonder why on earth anybody not under compulsion should go on living in London. This moment of speculation did not last long, because I did in fact then feel myself still under a compulsion of habit, curiosity, and supposed necessity.

Thinking of those vividly remembered moments of sudden and grateful immersion in country air and country silence puts me in mind of an observation by Norman Douglas. 'A retrospect of life', he wrote in his own flavoursome and well devised retro-spect, *Looking Back*, 'is a chain, a broken chain, of remembered moments.' Not a very fresh or striking image, but a true one where a wandering and fragmentary life is concerned. A diligent and regular diarist (I know of several now living) has no need of retrospect; he is constantly spinning his aide-mémoire. The non-diarist must shuffle through the snapshots capricious memory has fixed. He can only collect links or irregular strands of the broken chain.

So far as I was connected, or my relations and friends were connected, with places and regions, these were seldom remote or northerly. Escape from London was nearly always southward or westward. The Cotswolds, the Chilterns, the Thames Valley, South Wales, Kent, Surrey, and Sussex were the usual settings for chance groupings, glimpses of other people's lives and standards of taste, relaxed pleasures, sudden intimacies, and spontaneous confessions. Rooms opened on to gardens aloof from the car-infested roads. In quiet rooms, old gardens, and easy conversation there was healing and renewal.

I know more about Sussex gardens now than I did then. The arboretum at West Dean can hardly be called a garden; it is more like a secret entry into Nepal. Numb with wet moss, the hillside paths wind among banked or tree-tall shrubs; May switches on myriads of many-coloured rhododendrons and azaleas, and the luminous glades are suffused with a sleepy fragrance; for above them soar the stiff spires of giant rare conifers from Asia; turn a corner, and there, yes, surely, is a dak bungalow. May is also the time for Sir Frederick Stern's miraculous paradise in a chalk-pit at Highdown. But Rodmell has always seemed to me at its best in late summer, with the fig trees expansively southern, the pear trees weighted with abundance, the zinnias glowing in pure scarlet, yellow, and magenta, a heat haze over the valley of the Ouse at midday, and evening opalescence lending a nuance of autumn to Mount Caburn. In a workroom in that garden Virginia Woolf did much of her writing, overlooked (it seems a little ironic) by the tower of Rodmell Church.

Once at teatime indoors in the summer the click of the gate

was heard, and a second or two later there appeared in profile in one of the windows a stylish panama hat, sporting in cut and tilted slightly forward on a determined, military-looking head with a granite chin, the head itself set rigidly on a square, parade-ground chest and shoulders which, lacking epaulettes, looked un-dressed. At a glance one might have thought this the top part of a Prussian field-marshal just back from shooting chamois in the Carpathians. The purposeful progress of this animated bust, in vivid relief against the old yew hedge, and without a glance to left or right, was as resolute as that of some old man-of-war, called perhaps *Immitigable*, *Indomitable*, or *Impregnable*, carrying a great many guns and under urgent orders to ram and board a cornered enemy. But there was no enemy, this visitor was not on any hostile intent, and, just as a man-of-war used to be called *she*, was in fact of the feminine gender. The baton in her knapsack was more wandlike than that of a field-marshal; she was a com-poser; and the only English one with whom I was then acquainted.

As the figurehead, pressing on steadily towards the front door, appeared in a second and then a third window Virginia Woolf looked up and exclaimed, 'Good heavens, there's Ethel!' Her ex-clamation seemed to signify 'What fun!' and anybody who looks into the memoirs of Ethel Smyth can easily discern why. This high-spirited woman addressed herself to life with a gusto more often seen in her generation than in ours. If her sensibility had been as conspicuous as her energy, her music might have been as attractive as her enjoyment of life. Perhaps it is; but what I have heard of it has suggested to me collision and grappling irons and war cries, or repeated discharges of firearms in a Central European mountain landscape; the rocks reverberated, the knickerbockered field-marshal clapped his Zeiss glasses to his battlefield eyes, but there was never a sign of the nimble chamois; it had been too quick for the hunter.

She now snatched off her hat and cast it on to a table, revealing, clamped to her thinning grey hair (with which no coiffeur could be envisaged as having busied himself for some time), what looked like a headphone, as if on her way to Rodmell she had been determined not to miss a first performance, in Serbo-Croat at Zagreb, of *The Wreckers*. But the thing was only a device to alleviate impinging deafness.

'This damned contraption,' she cried in a tone of voice that cannot have been much like Beethoven's, 'is not the slightest good!'

And she snatched it off and flung it beside her hat. As I turned to follow her I noticed that the gesture had cost her a sizeable wisp or hank of grey hairs, which had been caught in a joint of the contraption as she wrenched it from her scalp, without, so to speak, turning a hair. A moment later, she and Virginia Woolf were seated knee to knee and tête-à-tête on a couple of upright chairs. The composer had a lot to say. The writer was almost immediately speechless, because laughter, uncontrollable laughter, had taken possession of her. She quivered, she vibrated; every time she attempted to speak, her throat seemed to close up, and she touched it with one of her beautiful long hands as if to free herself from choking.

'But, Ethel—' she said, and got no further. Tears of laughter coursed down her face, while the composer, as sure of this good listener as of an orchestra in full cry, unswervingly pursued her theme. . . .

Summer in Sussex, summer in Surrey—that part of it which faces south from the slopes between Guildford and Dorking. In a William Morris-papered bedroom a brass can of hot water, covered with a face towel to keep it hot, waits patiently in the basin on the washstand. Time to wash, yes, but how to stop looking out of the window of this quiet house at that quiet view? Such things are not to be enjoyed in London: those who enable one to enjoy them in the country are more than friends, they are lifegivers. The late hot afternoon light gives an almost African look to Hackhurst Down and its old wild black yew trees of the Pilgrims' Way, and the heat has drawn out from the flower-covered cistus bushes beyond the lawn a Mediterranean fragrance, suggesting goats, rocks, and lizards. The peaceful warmth seems deepened by the passage of an airborne stag-beetle on a drowsy cruise towards the wood.

Downstairs Mrs Forster, the novelist's mother, is sitting near a window facing south. She is overlooked by the Richmond drawing of her son's great-aunt, Marianne Thornton. It is earlier in the afternoon, or it is another afternoon in an earlier or later year, and from the window can be seen a flourishing tree-of-heaven, and further off, down at the end of the sloping garden, the distant figure of Bone, the gardener, stooping among the raspberry canes. Perhaps the novelist is only a young man, perhaps this is the nineteenth century still, or the early twentieth (which is much the same thing), when ladies sit in drawing-rooms with silver spirit kettles and cakestands, sit quietly recalling the past and noticing the present instead of rushing about. The door opens, admitting Agnes with the tea. Thin, kindly, and formal, she wears the light armour-plating of a parlourmaid, her perceptibly starched cuffs and apron and the biretta-like cap on the top of her head all dead white, all crackling faintly like the talc of a dragonfly's wings. It might almost be teatime at my grandmother's in Buxton in 1909, the tempo is so tranquil and the atmosphere so much one of safe-seeming, immortal-seeming seclusion. Mrs Forster and Agnes seem to have their being in a perspective that shuts out the great garish world and greatly magnifies details in the foreground. Some discussion was held between them earlier today about the precise whereabouts, colour, and function of a pencil; it was conducted with a quiet care and stately thoroughness that suggested conformity with an almost Confucian system of order and appropriateness.

The tea ceremony is certainly in the style of 1909, but the small wireless set at Mrs Forster's elbow is not—nor is her son, who presently comes into the room. He brings with him anything but a feeling of troubling this peace: he is part of it. The house was designed and built by his father. It is his home (this word has special potency for the nomad guest) and there can be no question that he loves it. In 1909 he was already a novelist, but if his early novels are charged with an aroma of their time, they are charged also (the point need not be laboured) with the dynamite of non-acceptance. This is his home, but he is only intermittently here; he belongs to the world and the present, to the future too; he is a harbinger of change.

In this last half-century of violent and in some ways total change it has sometimes been more than usually the mark of a superior understanding not to be what my father used to call a stick-in-the-mud, not to get stuck with any rigid formula of life or belief but to show curiosity about change, enough adaptability at least to recognize it, and enough understanding to discriminate between its fertilizing and its transitory or stultifying tendencies. Curiosity, adaptability, and independence are some of the qualities that have kept E. M. Forster in touch with quite other aspects of the world than this, his mother's drawing room in Surrey. But it is something much more, the undefinable motive power of his personality, that has put him in revolt against much in his time and enabled him to follow his negatives with a positive creed, attitude, and theory of conduct. I have heard superficial people praise or condemn his early writings for 'period charm' or for 'dating a bit'; they were too stupid to recognize the direct blasts of a mind that has sometimes worked like a flame-thrower, scorching up some falsity held to be truth. Unfortunately falsity grows again, however often it is cut down.

The small tabby cat at my feet, I notice as I drink my tea, has a wry neck. I ask if this is a natural deformity or the result of an accident.

'Poor Toma,' he says, 'had a stroke. It happened while he was listening to a broadcast of *The Flying Dutchman.* . . .'

And now it is November, at a farmhouse in Wharfedale. My host's father, telling me what a lot of rabbits there are on the fell, says, 'On a summer's evening you can see millions of them. If you clap your hands, why, you'd think the blessed earth was moving.' Language is not often so perfectly used by non-literary persons. Hearing us speak of Haworth, he unexpectedly says, 'Ah, Haworth. That was where they raked the moon out of the pond, so they used to say when I was a lad.' This was not a joke about the Brontës, who were no more than a name to him, but just a stale country whimsy.

His son, Norman Carr, took me to see Haworth. No day could have been more propitious. It was November, and the climate gave us the full treatment. We drove off after lunch in semi-darkness and a wind that was strong, damp, and piercingly cold. The clouds were low, tearing along with maniac speed over the austere, deserted fells and stained the same sapless tint as the withered heather. This deepened to a depressive dark grey with tinges of puce and khaki, as if the clouds were the effluence of Satanic mills not far away; and then there would be a sudden, livid, whitish area among them, as if some horrible flare were being dropped above. For an instant everything was blurred by rain; a few gritty handfuls of small hailstones were flung contemptuously against the windscreen; then these turned soft and were seen to be sleet. After this we drove without surprise into a swirling theatrical fog, not very thick but of an uncommonly sulphurous khaki colour. By the time we reached Keighley the fog had dispersed and the wind had gone down a little; the sky had turned blackish, and a few chilled and rugged souls, hunched under shawls and black umbrellas, were scurrying along, as if to sit for early drawings by Van Gogh.

To find a funeral procession preceding us up the hill to Haworth was a real stroke of what in the theatre is called production, on the part of Fate. We were obliged to slow down and follow it. Anything more stagy can hardly be imagined. The pathetic fallacy was working overtime: the sky loured and threatened, the wind wailed and wuthered, gutters wept copiously. A mournful bell was tolling from the church, and before we got to the Black Bull soft, squashy flakes of snow had begun to fall. As soon as they touched the glossy black roof of the hearse they dissolved and ran down it like the tears of an Ethiopian princess.

We had the immortal house to ourselves. The silence and semi-darkness and solitude left the body free to manœuvre in those haunted rooms and the imagination free to try and enter into those lives that had flared up in them and given out an unprecedented radiance, now light-years away. The window of the room on the ground floor which had been Charlotte Brontë's husband's study was framed in ivy leaves as black and shiny as patent leather. It looked straight into the churchyard, the surface of which was well above the level of the floor, and the thought of the very juices of mortality seeping almost into the foundations of the house was not wholly comforting.

I will not swear that I caught sight in Haworth of a teashop called Emily's Pantry, but I was credibly informed that in summer months a great many trippers were conveyed to the place in motor coaches marked 'Brontë Tours Ltd.' It is very easy to deplore the commercialization of a place with such associations and of the memory of the rare spirits who gave rise to them, but such is fame. Foreign visitors apart, Stratford-on-Avon may be presumed to be visited by semi-educated hordes of litter-droppers, but perhaps such people are part of the backbone of this industrialized England. If one does not care for the sight of vertebrae, or of other people enjoying themselves, one can always stay away; but it is priggish to condemn and impossible to prevent their attempting to improve their understandings of the environment and civilization in which the most eminent of Englishmen long ago exerted himself. . . .

The scene changes to Tiger Bay, the dockside quarter of Cardiff, and, by a slight transition, to a 'depressed area' in the mining valleys behind it. I would not say that nothing but a hope of self-improvement took me there; curiosity has in it an element of pleasure. Among its rewards were evidences of Welsh temperament and Welsh brains triumphing wonderfully over unemployment, and varieties of night life in strong chiaroscuro and with crude musical accompaniment, suggesting dramatic waterfronts in French films. In Wales, as in Ireland, it was possible to feel very far from England; there were moments of total foreignness.

To Ireland I went, to visit Elizabeth Bowen at Bowen's Court, and as the boat from Fishguard slowly made its way up the estuary towards Cork, the light mists that dangled or drifted over the trees seemed sub-tropical. The disposition of the landscape, and the colourwashed houses, pale pink, blue, or buff, and the stray fishing boats on the silky water, and the men in them, and the cormorants on the buoys, suggested an approach to a remote island. A pink ruin glided by, as if on a pivot. It was said to have been a hotel. But there were no numbers now on the bedroom doors, because there were no bedroom doors. On the long road by the shore two or three cars passed; across the water one could hear the swishing sound of the tyres on the moist asphalt until it grew fainter and ceased. Throbbing gently, the boat passed a sham medieval tower at the water's edge It was inhabited, and a young man was leaning against it and smoking a cigarette. He wore no raincoat in spite of the wetting mist, and looked at the boat as one might look at a passing cloud. If he had been an Englishman he would have been indoors or would already have gone busily off somewhere, instead of standing by himself in the cool, quiet, early morning air; but this was Ireland.

At school in England the history of this country, this producer of wits, poets, heroes, beauties, and (let us admit it) bores, had not been properly taught to us. It had either been ignored, glossed over, or given an Orange tinge. St Patrick got rid of the snakes, and after some time Cromwell arrived to 'crush the rebels' and establish 'law and order'. Shortly afterwards William III won the Battle of the Boyne. But it happened that Easter Week, the Sinn Fein ideal, and the fate of Casement had made a strong impression upon my boyish imagination. As I grew older I wondered whether the ignorance, prejudice, intolerance, injustice, folly, famine, and violence that seemed to have accompanied the English occupation of Ireland had been wholly necessary. In other parts of the world, too, the English, instead of trying to understand the feelings of other peoples, have labelled them 'rebels' or 'terrorists' and brought force to bear upon them in the name of 'law and order'. My Uncle William, who commanded the Royal Irish Fusiliers, once explained to me the military advantages of combining Irish dash with English moderation. Why, I wondered, did it have to be a *military* combination?

Often in Ireland a dwelling and a ruin stand side by side, and often the ruin stands alone — a roofless mill, full of young trees instead of machinery; or an old tower in a cloud of ivy; or a wayside or upland cabin; or a great burnt mansion of early nineteenth-century Gothic with bunches of twisted waterpipes sticking out of it like severed arteries; or a mouldering police barracks looking haunted behind overgrown hedges of flowering fuchsia, with the apple tree near it in which a sniper was once sniped. Another ruin — Bridgetown Abbey beside the Blackwater, its grey stone turning a darker grey when the rain wets it. It is approached by a lane overgrown with brambles weighed down by fat blackberries that nobody picks, the Blackwater glides over its dark rocky bed, and trees on a cliff catch the afternoon light. Masonry has fallen, and lies where it fell; weeds have sprung up, and a few nineteenth-century graves in a roofless chapel keep company with old tombs. From the side of one of these a stone slab has fallen, inside it lies flat an old thick oaken board which was once the side of a coffin, and there is the skeleton of its occupant; through the pelvis a nettle has thrust, and is now in flower. Such a sight would not be lawful in England, or orderly.

Across the meadows to what is left of the castle of Kilcolman, where Spenser lived, wrote, empire-built, and rebel-crushed. The bog water reflects a livid evening sky, and the haycocks cast long lilac shadows on the grass. The place is sometimes visited by consumptives from a sanatorium not far away. One of them has torn up a letter and thrown the fragments on the ground, and some phrases, in very clear writing, shape themselves on the grass in the headstrong hopefulness of consumptives:

'. . . she was hoping . . . said I would never . . . last time darling . . . looking forward more than ever . . .'

Not a ruin, but more desolate than a ruin, is a great lead-coloured house, closed up, deserted, some of its windows shuttered and some not, with black-shadowed ilex thickets and overgrown lawns of a green so vivid that it hurts the eyes, with stalactites beginning to form under the heraldic pediment, and a solitary donkey nibbling the grass between the paving stones in the yard outside the coach house. These country houses, often extravagantly built and standing in walled demesnes, were the breeding places of that gifted race, the Anglo-Irish. 'The most brilliant and charming people in the world,' a travelled old Englishman had told me. 'One day last summer,' he said, 'when I was staying over there at a perfectly delightful house, hip baths were brought out on to the lawn and filled with cushions, and we sat in them all the afternoon drinking port and eating gooseberries. Such hospitality! Such conversation!'

Such conversation, yes, among all the Irish, with their seductive voices and brogue, but their enthusiastic monologues can be wonderfully fatiguing. Ireland is a heavenly country to visit, but might be less heavenly to live in. It is so melancholy, so full of the ghosts of feuds and famines, the clouds fly low, the trees sag under the incessant rain, and the very air seems charged with a sense of grievance. How could one keep out the climate, how could one keep the Pope and Ulster at a proper distance, except by settling in Rome or London, taking to drink, or cutting one's throat? I felt then that there was still scope for a Gogol to go round in a car, on some pretext that would appeal to vanity or cupidity, and visit the surviving denizens of the demesnes up and down the country. What material for a novel that will now never be written! I think Turgeniev said it was the example of Miss Edgeworth that gave him the impetus to write about his own people. There were certainly parallels between pre-republican Russia and pre-republican Ireland, and a Russian reader might enjoy *The Absentee* as much as an Irish reader might enjoy *Dead Souls*. And still, in the Thirties, with the remains of a landowning class and the survival of a peasantry, Russia was brought nearer, the nineteenth and the eighteenth century too.

These impressions I owed to my brilliant friend and hostess at Bowen's Court, and among them the image of a very small lake in the hills beyond Killarney, as clear as a dewdrop, with a tumbledown pale-blue inn and a few pine trees beside it. In the pure air a spotlight of sunshine travels slowly across the scene, giving it an almost supernatural beauty. A hillock of wet grass glows in the sun like an emerald, there is no sound but the Yeatsian lapping of the lake water, a tuft of flowering heather looks like something precious, and as a background to it all the sombre mountains are slowly suffused with the colour and bloom of damsons. They seem to grow taller and gloomier and more Ossianic as their impossibly deep purple deepens still further, and the darkening clouds pass over them trailing mile-long scarves of gauzy rain. A faint seethe of sound is audible even from here. It is going to pour again. It has begun.

I I

Marine Residences

WHY was I drawn back to the sea? Was it simply that the whole metabolism of one 'long in city pent' needed refreshment so badly that he was driven by hunger for clean air as a man may be driven by a craving for food or drink? Or was it the return of an addict to the drug of swimming and the lulled balance of well-being that may follow swimming, especially when one lies idly in the sun? Or was it simply that to a modern, urbanized man, who had lived some of his earliest and intensest years far from anything like a town, it seemed necessary to live for a time, if in a town, at least in a town with a permanent and very large open space on one side? Not that one can love the sea. It may soothe by its calmness, impress by its radiance or majesty, its power and noise, or attract as the element over which one sails or hunts for fish. But it is oppressively elemental, and a great fidget.

It is often supposed that English seaside towns are depressing. For the greater part of the year, it is alleged, they are chilly, wet, and dark, with a deserted, out-of-season air, no 'life' either indoors or out, and no society in which a man of feeling or taste can pleasurably mix. During the short summer season they are believed to be made intolerable by moronic swarms of 'holiday makers' or trippers ignorant of the possible graces of living, equally indifferent to nature and the arts, to good cooking, wine, conversation, music, or books, to the true pleasures of either society or solitude, wasting their time, overtiring the noisy and badly brought up children they call 'the kiddies', spending a lot of money, and getting less for it, as a French friend of mine used to say, than they would anywhere else in the world. I see that it is possible to take such a view, but if it had been mine I should have stayed away from English seaside towns or gone elsewhere. The two seaside towns that drew me had each a character quite its own, and in each I found it possible to live an agreeable and free sort of life.

I spent one long summer in Dover, which I cannot claim to have 'discovered'. Whatever it is like now, it had then both charm and atmosphere. People elsewhere were generally astonished to learn that one had chosen to remain there for months on end. They regarded Dover as no more than part of the pipeline that took vast numbers of people back and forth between England and the rest of Europe. And yet one could live pleasantly there. A friend of mine had been in the habit of taking a flat in one of the comfortable old-fashioned houses overlooking the harbour. At the open windows on summer evenings it was pleasant to sit with a drink and stare at the calm sea. There were no trippers, there was no traffic, and the caterwauling of seagulls, for which the cliffs acted as a sounding board, added a touch of melancholy to the atmosphere. Occasionally a phrase or flourish of military music from the castle far above floated down for effect, and in the evenings the streets, very quiet in the daytime, were filled with the inaudible frou-frou of kilts, as the young soldiers of the garrison made their way to the pubs.

There was one good restaurant, where I sometimes dined. I used to lunch at a small commercial hotel, where the food was surprisingly good. My attendance being unexplained, I was known there (I found out by chance) as 'Mr X'. Even more enigmatic was one of my fellow lunchers, an oldish woman. Every day she came into the dining room at a quarter to one, looking rather pixilated under a mop of 'iron grey' hair, bobbed in the style of the Twenties. She wore slippers, and a speckled dress like the plumage of a faded guineafowl, and carried a large leather bag stuffed with unknown possessions; it was heavy. She invariably sat down to a breakfast of two boiled eggs, and ate them with much fussiness, daintiness, and quick, bird-like movements. As soon as she had finished she was provided with a pint-sized jug of hot water, which she carried with her out of the room, for some unknown purpose. Exactly half an hour later she returned for lunch, which always consisted of fish. Although in perfect health she had not been out of the house for a year. She used to spend all her time alone in her room, but it was known that she did not sew, or read, or write, and that she had no wireless. What did she do in there? What was in that bag? Sometimes she read *John Bull* over her fish, a paper that in those days specialized in exposing frauds and abuses. It might be, to judge by her furtive eyes and whisperings, that she saw life and the world as one vast confidence trick. Perhaps she was right; perhaps her bag contained the secret of the universe. . . . No concern of hers, it seemed, the rise of Hitler, the Spanish Civil War, the China Incident, the invasion of Abyssinia. Snug as a woodlouse, she would hardly have regarded them as realities.

One afternoon I walked over to Kingsdown. A strong wind patterned the sea with curly white waves. The sea was streaked with loud blues and greens, and the wind prevented the fishing boats from making headway; with their cigar-brown sails they dipped and fluttered, like moths in glue. Everything was movement at this windswept corner of England, nothing was progress. The waves broke and whitened as far as the eye could see, the sailing-boats rocked and tilted and got no further, the grass on the cliff streamed along the ground but stuck to its roots. At Kingsdown there were villas not yet opened for the summer, and the shuttered beach huts, their paint faded by sun and salt, had an air of secrecy, as if a crime had been committed in one of them. Between the houses and the huts was a shingle flat a hundred yards wide, where masses of pink valerian had run wild. It was all in flower, dancing against the clean buff shingle and the peacocking sea.

I came back a different way, passing one of those deserted military follies that occur in what is left of the English landscape, a town of ruined concrete huts overgrown with elder bushes and nettles, a refuge for tramps (there were still tramps in those days), courting couples, and idle boys. Further on was a deep valley where grew the fragrant, the pyramidal, the bee, and the spider orchises, and where once, in thundery weather, I picked a bouquet of mixed flowers with several sorts of butterflies firmly attached, too drowsy to fly away.

This region was a haunt of Harry Houchen, a casual acquaintance. He had been coming there ever since he was a child. Before he married he used to bring his girl there, but now she would not come because there was always so much to do at home, so he sometimes brought one of his own children to tumble about and pick dandelions or blackberries. Harry himself had a taste for seagulls' eggs, which he collected on the cliffs; he gathered mushrooms, snared rabbits, or lay in the sun, smoking. He owned a boat, which could be seen from the top of the cliff, moored far below, and sometimes went fishing. His clothes were ragged, and he seemed more cheerful and contented than almost anybody I knew. He had the advantage of not living in a totalitarian State, and of not being ashamed of being idle or of enjoying himself.

'I had my great chance,' he said one day, smiling at his thigh, which could be seen through a rent in his old trousers, 'and if I'd taken it I wouldn't have been like this now.'

It had happened that when he was seventeen or eighteen Harry was serving in a smallish boat engaged in coastal trade varied with occasional voyages to Holland and Belgium. In Belgium the captain had an acquaintance, a middle-aged bachelor who owned three shops, a tailor's, a barber's, and a restaurant. He was an anglophile and wished to adopt a young Englishman to help him in the conduct of the three businesses and to be a companion to him. He said that if the young man turned out well he would make him his heir: could the captain recommend anybody? The captain recommended Harry Houchen, and Harry was installed. But the boy could not manage to learn Flemish; he was looked askance at because he was a foreigner; and in spite of the kindness of his patron he found that after three months he could bear his exile no longer. So one night he crept out of the house, joined a boat, and returned to England and his old haunts.

'And is it *all* gravel?' an American visitor wistfully asked me, looking at the shingly, shelving beach. It was a windless morning for once. The sea was perfectly calm, a milky green. Smoke, blackish or yellowish, coiling from a thin and distant funnel here and there, seemed to enter the waiting air and spread like some dark substance injected into a vein. Far away to the right a fog signal in the heat haze made a noise like a cow deprived of her calf; far away to the left a dredger was clanking and creaking in the outer harbour. In the garden not a leaf moved, the curtains hung motionless at the windows, and the girl who was sitting on the balcony put down her sewing and looked out to sea, but it was impossible to tell where the sea ended and the sky began.

Suddenly the sun came out, and all the bathing children became children of light. Three very fair and slender little girls in pale blue, pale yellow, and white bathing suits hovered at the water's edge, and people sat on the shingle and idled in boats, like figures in that great *Baignade* by Seurat. A boy with red bathing drawers waded into the sea and stood, with the water up to his waist, gazing at the horizon. His biscuit-coloured torso, apparently severed from the rest of him, rested on the calm surface as if on a sheet of glass. Attention was attracted by a small, splashing figure in shallow water: I immediately recognized it as Elsie. Attention was something she was constituted to attract.

I had first got to know Elsie a couple of weeks earlier, when I was sunbathing one morning on the then lonely and so-called Shakespeare beach. I was approached by a young girl who asked me if I would guard her clothes while she bathed, but I could not imagine anybody wanting to steal them. She rapidly undressed beside me, talking and giggling as she did so, and then sat down, still uncovered above the waist. Finding that I took little notice of her (to one with my Afro-Asian past, naked little girls were no novelty) she made for the water, buttoning up her bathing suit as she went. Her bathing consisted of ostentatious floundering in the shallow water a few yards from my feet, and her movements were punctuated with loud cries of delight and invitation. When she came out she talked incessantly, and presently came to the point.

'Where do you live?' she asked.

'Over there,' I replied.

'Is your wife there?'

'No.'

'Why not?'

'Because I haven't got a wife.'

'Do you live with your Mum?'

'No.'

'Who looks after you?'

'Oh, various people.'

'Wouldn't you like me to look after you?'

'Thanks, but I'm very well looked after.'

'Who do you sleep with?'

'It depends.'

'Do you sleep alone?'

'Sometimes.'

'Don't you get lonely when you sleep alone?'

'Not a bit.'

'Wouldn't you like to sleep with me?'

'You'd never stop talking.'

'What would you do if I walked into the bathroom when you were having a bath, and you were standing up and facing the door?'

'I always sit down in my bath, but it's quite likely I might tell you to buzz off and not be so nosy.'

'Wouldn't you like to marry me?'

'Not today, thank you.'

'What's your name?'

'Mickey Mouse.'

'Oh . . .! You fibber! Oh, what a fib! God is listening to you. How can you tell such fibs when God can hear us?'

'I'm sure God has a great many more interesting things to listen to.'

'Oh . . .'

'By the way,' I said pleasantly, 'why don't you go and drown yourself?'

'Would you rescue me?'

'Certainly not.'

'But don't you like me?'

'You talk such a lot.'

At Home

'Would you like me if I didn't talk so much?'

'I doubt it. But I can't answer any more questions today.'

The sun was nice and warm, and I lay back and closed my eyes. Elsie began to balance stones along my outstretched arm, arranged others in patterns on my chest, and then, giggling delightedly, began to build a little cairn on a more personal foundation.

'Now, now,' I said . . .

Elsie undoubtedly had a future; Lady Chalkham lived in the past. The first time I went to see her she noticed that I was looking at a framed photograph.

'A tremendous beauty, isn't she? It's Princess Eudoxia. She used to stay with us before the war.'

I saw a young woman in radiant health, straight backed, with her hair in a bang, a high bust, and her satin hips so smoothly corseted that she looked like a fish. *To dear Ada*, ran the inscription, *Cordially, Eudoxia Victoria of Blundenburg-Stettin*. And what a handwriting! What energy! What confidence! Lady Chalkham herself must have looked like that. She too was a product of all kinds of lucky chances and patient cultivations, a perfect specimen of a kind of woman that would never be produced again. I imagined an early environment not without stateliness, in which convention allowed for playfulness; but it is now difficult to gauge the incredible innocence in which, like many women of her class and generation, she had married.

Somewhere there must be an early photograph of herself yearning towards the camera, her head turned over a bare shoulder thrust up from a fuzz of tulle like an egg emerging from the fluffy recesses of a hen. It might have prompted one to evoke, one by one, little scenes from her past, each with its convention of clothes and behaviour, its special setting and companions, successive phases in the long evolution of a personality. I see her as a young woman reclining in a punt, with a Japanese fan in her hand, wearing balloon sleeves of broderie anglaise, and a hard straw hat tilted over bright eyes fixed on a young man in a tall hard collar and narrow white flannels; sitting at a dressing table with silver-backed brushes and a little book of papier poudré, lifting her soft arms so that the loose sleeves fall back from the elbows, and slowly going through that beautiful lost movement, slowly withdrawing the long, jewel-headed pins from a huge hat heaped up with white roses; gathering up her skirts in one hand as she crosses the road, and then pausing to consult a watch suspended over her left breast from a diamond brooch in the form of a bow; peppering the backs of postcards (views of Venice, Cairo, or St Petersburg) with exclamation marks; seeing poverty at a distance or Naples through a porthole; watching the slow-motioned withdrawal of Alps, vast, useless, and dazzling, from the steamy windows of a railway carriage; settling a feather boa round a lace collar supported with stiffeners, stepping with cardcase and parasol into a carriage to pay calls, and driving off between banks of ferns in a smell of horses; bathing at Biarritz in waterlogged black serge with white pipings; going motoring in an ulster, thickly veiled, perched high above the ground, and moving off with a jerk in a cloud of blue vapour among respectful but sceptical onlookers, who step back in alarm as the machine snorts by; attending weddings, funerals, garden parties, musical evenings; appearing on lawns, the decks of yachts, racecourses; playing diabolo, bezique, puss in the corner; arriving at a tango tea, wearing a small hat adorned with sweeping ospreys, carrying a flat leopard skin muff as square as the top of a table, and hardly able to put one foot before the other because of the tightness of the skirt above the ankles, a skirt split upward from the hem for four inches, attention being called to this provocative opening by two red buttons as big as half-crowns. A little later she follows the fashions of the early war-years, going out in a plumed shako, a frogged coat, a tent-shaped skirt well off the ground, and high laced boots. It seems only the other day that she passed laughing, to the music of Suppé, under a striped awning to a sunlit lawn; and then she found herself bending graciously over wounded soldiers in beds, a little troubled by the mingled smell of men, flannel, and iodoform. The time of wounds had come.

It was easy, it was not false, to see her in these fashionplate terms. It was not false, but it only made a type of her, not an individual. I looked out of her drawing room, through the french windows into the rainy garden, where the fuchsia bushes were hung with coral pendants and each pendant was covered with sliding raindrops, and I thought sadly how easy it is to falsify the past with generalizations, romantic fables, with envy, ignorance, and prejudice. I did know enough, as it happened, about Lady Chalkham to see below the gracious surface; I knew there had been turmoil and suffering, and something of its nature. These were the Thirties: I knew they would seem remote in thirty years' time—falsified, romanticized, despised for their weaknesses and absurdities. The Nineties, in which Lady Chalkham had been a young woman, were cheaply referred to as 'gay' or 'naughty'. I doubt if they were any more or less gay or naughty than any other period, except that wealth and over-confidence allowed some kinds of people in some ways to be frivolous and irresponsible—but so does poverty and insecurity, if they are bent that way.

I happened to have made some investigation into life at Dover in the Nineties. Naturally there were gaieties of sorts, public or private, open or secret; naturally the over-confident note of jingo imperialism floated down in bugle calls from the Castle above the

off-white cliffs; but all was not beer and skittles. Religious
activities played a large part in the life of the town. Meetings were
continually being held by missionary societies, Bands of Hope,
synods, Lord's Day Observance societies, and similar bodies;
'sacred concerts' were frequent, and much was made of 'a three-
days' conference on the Second Coming'. The English love of
minding other people's business was being indulged, and meetings
were held 'in support of the persecuted Armenians'. The English
capacity to 'feel for woes beyond the wave' may be a good thing
but in the last century, as in this, charity did not always begin at
home; and Ebenezer Elliott had perhaps been right to complain,
even if in bad verse, at the readiness of the pious in his day to send
Bibles to the heathen and 'bacon to the Jews'.

> Their lofty souls have telescopic eyes,
> Which see the smallest speck of distant pain,
> While, at their feet, a world of agonies,
> Unseen, unheard, unheeded, writhes in vain.

I don't think there was a world of agonies in Dover in the mid-
Nineties, but it was disquieting to learn of the apparent prevalence
of suicide among the working class, with its suggestion of less
public agonies. An engine driver cut his throat; a baker threw
himself from the western heights 'during a state of temporary
insanity'; a maidservant 'was killed by falling over the cliff', two
bottles of a drug being found where she fell; a bootmaker was
found dead on the downs 'with a half full bottle of poison beside
him'; an artilleryman 'shot himself and died immediately'; and a
messenger boy 'died from taking carbolic acid' among those
bramble thickets which were a haunt of Harry Houchen's. Two
seamen were committed to prison for refusing to serve in a
steamer that took the Prince of Wales to France. Why? On

political or moral grounds? Social history is more complex than it is sometimes made out to be.

My attention to the social history of Dover as it was being made around me, and by me, was diverted a little by a book I was editing for publication. It was by Haruko Ichikawa, the wife of a professor at the Imperial University in Tokyo, with whom I had been acquainted. With him she had done a tour of Europe, subsidized by an American foundation. She had kept a travel diary; this had been translated into English, and it appeared here as *Japanese Lady in Europe*. 'Unsophisticated sensibility as on a photographic film unmarked with any preconceived ideas' was the state of mind Mrs Ichikawa had aimed at, and it gave her book a flavour of its own. She and her husband 'often spoke unkindly' of the English for being 'stolid' or 'too composed', but when it was time to leave she felt a slight pang. It was the only European country that had that effect upon her: she felt, so she wrote, that she had left here about a fiftieth part of her soul. 'Stolid tenacity and obtuse stubbornness' were, in the eyes of Natsume Soseki, peculiarly English qualities. That eminent Japanese writer spent three years in this country at the beginning of the century. His teeth seem to have been set on edge by English genteelness.

'Gentleman!' he wrote. 'What is a gentleman? Who is a gentleman? The most ungentlemanlike English people never tire of harping on this everlasting string.' Elsewhere he wrote:

Go to England to see what is meant by good manners. They say this is nice, that is nice. Everything seems to them nice enough. Strange to say, however, it is those who use the word most that do not know its meaning. Go along dirty streets of London, and you may pick up any quantity of 'nice'. There is no place where 'nice' is sold at such a cheap rate and in such abundance. And what for? Merely to please others! They do not know a person may be offended by being called nice by those who do not know what 'nice' is.

Was this just the bitterness of a young man from the Far East isolated in London? If so, he was not the last to feel it.

My other, and later, marine residence was at Brighton, where I lived for the best part of two years in the later Thirties. It was right in the very middle of the town, between the two piers, not far from the sea, and what estate agents call perfectly secluded; a small house in one of those alleyways—or 'twittens' as they are traditionally called in Sussex—known as 'the Lanes' and famous for their antique shops and junk shops. No wheeled traffic could pass my door, and in bed late at night it was often pleasant to listen to the dwindling tattoo of the belated footsteps of a passerby. It put me in mind, for some reason, of Thomas Hardy, and so, sometimes, did other aspects of Brighton (he spent, by the way, his first honeymoon there). At the back, the house opened on to an enclosed garden, not overlooked, not large certainly, and wonderfully isolated, sheltered against the rampaging southwesterly gales, and open in a proper summer to the blessed sun for many hours a day. A few steps from this unexpected little hideout one could be in the full hurly-burly of Brighton. It is only a suburb of London but was agreeable to live in, especially in the winter.

My landlord was of what used to be called humble origins. He told me he had grown prosperous by diligently writing what he called 'mush' for the twopenny weeklies for women. He had also a serious side, and assured me that he had read fourteen times a book by Middleton Murry called, quite bluntly, *God*. I did not urge him to enlarge upon this addiction.

At Home

I had taken the place furnished. Everything in the life of a nomad is conditional, particularly when there are men like Hitler, Mussolini, and Stalin in the ascendant. I did not know how long I intended to stay, and I had for years been careful to avoid accumulating possessions. I had not particularly noticed the furniture; it seemed serviceable and was clean and adequately comfortable. I might perhaps have foreseen the horrified reaction of Herbert Read when he stepped into one of my rooms and found himself confronted with a piece of ill-designed machine-made furniture. After one glance on first arriving, I had ignored it. I had now no inclination to defend it, but after hearing my visitor's exclamations and seeing his expression of horror, like something in a picture by Fuseli, I rapidly tried to improvise some excuse for allowing it to share my habitat. I believe, by the way, that I may be the only man living who has said to him, perhaps with more courage than mischievousness, and in, of all places, a severe London gallery hung with still more severe abstract paintings, 'But Herbert, why can't *every* picture tell a story?' It is a wonder I am alive to record this: he is not such a mild man as he looks.

12

The Typewritten Word

M y temperament and talent did not impel me to try and make a living by writing books; they impelled me to write books only when I wished and only of whatever kind I wished. Though startled, and naturally gratified, by the comparative success of *The Case is Altered*, I could not imagine myself turning into a novelist of regular habits, whether a popular one or an unpopular one. Literature has its battery hens; I was a wilder fowl. The history of modern literature abounded with instances of novelists of great or of more than ordinary gifts who had written too much and too often, struggling to support themselves and their families, more or less embittered by want of the recognition and income they felt they deserved, haunted by fears of a drying-up of their inventiveness, a trial to their dependants, and liable to lose their own as well as other people's esteem. It was not so much prudence that kept me from adding to their number as the lack of a sense of vocation as a whole-time storyteller. I have stuck to my intention to write fiction deliberately not constantly, and when I published my fifth novel I noticed with mild astonishment that eighteen years had passed since the appearance of my fourth. In the interval I had produced other books in prose and verse.

During the Thirties, when printing and publishing were much cheaper and easier than they are today, there seemed to be, as there seem still to be, many authors no better than mere bookmakers. Many men and women of mediocre capacity used to manufacture an annual novel. By dint of repetition and with luck many of them made some kind of name for themselves, obtained the notice of reviewers, and created some kind of demand, or at least a lack of resistance, among subscribers to the circulating libraries. Some made a living, some pocket money only. Most of them gave their real or hoped-for public what they thought it wanted or found it would accept. Among them were many purveyors of various grades of what my Brighton landlord called 'mush', but they were often less honest about it than he was, and deluded themselves that their mush was something of value. If mush is to be defined, perhaps it may be called the kind of writing which titillates the least exacting kinds of reader by appealing to the cheaper and shallower emotions—easy lust, sentimentality, or excitability—and by flattering uncultivated understandings, ignorance, prejudice, self-complacency, and accepted ideas. The mush-mongers are as active as ever, and there is no shortage of the titillant reading which in Afrikaans is called *prikkel-lektuur*.

Young men who wish to write are sometimes advised to earn their livings in some way that has nothing whatever to do with writing. They are urged to go out into the world, to travel, and earn their livings as they go, and learn about life in spheres unknown to them. If they have had a narrow, conventional upbringing and have not been about at all, this may be good advice. But constant changes of environment and a variety of experience in the first thirty years of my life inclined me now to the world of writers and writing. If a man's breadwinning work is akin to what he regards as the work for which he is best fitted it may keep him in training, broaden his technical knowledge, and develop his command of the medium he works in: Blake got his bread as a hack engraver. I saw no reason to shrink from reviewing, broadcasting, or editing, and having since those days had a good deal to do with these activities I regard them as a useful part of that process of education which for a writer is continuous. A devotee of the written word, and not without critical as well as creative tendencies, I was out to learn as much as I could about it, by reading as well as writing; so when Edward Garnett ceased to act as literary adviser to a conspicuous firm of publishers and I was invited to take his place, I did not immediately recoil in alarm and distaste.

I was acquainted with Edward Garnett, and I remember his showing me some photographs in which he appeared as a young man. They showed his noticeably fine hands, and I remarked on them.

'Oh yes,' he said, with perhaps a touch of natural pride in a good feature, 'those are the family hands.'

They seemed to me the reverse of grasping or ambitious; they showed refinement rather than suggested initiative; they were shapely, not *shaping*. I think it is true to say that he was a man in whom the critical faculty quite outweighed the creative, but that he had shown himself creatively critical, notably in his friendships with writers of the calibre of Conrad, the fineness of Hudson, and the worthiness of Galsworthy, as well as in the encouragement of lesser talents. The husband of Constance Garnett, whose translations from the Russian — whatever idiosyncrasies they may show — had opened up new worlds of the imagination to readers of English, and the father of David Garnett, he had a distinction of his own.

I did not take the invitation lightly, and accepted it with some diffidence. My critical faculty, though sometimes misused through a want of charity or good sense, had not been disused; I had for some years exercised it publicly in the regular conduct of a page of fiction reviews in the *Spectator*, as well as in occasional literary criticism, private as well as public. To advise an established and eminent firm of publishers how to invest their money, especially in my ignorance of the mechanics and finance of publishing, seemed at least as great a responsibility as advising casual readers of a politico-literary weekly what not to read in their spare time. I knew I had much to learn, and set myself to learn it; and I can honestly say that from the beginning I wrote full and conscientious reports on the material submitted to my judgment. Not on all of it, naturally, nor even on most of it, because most of it was either unsuitable, trivial, or worthless. But wherever there had been a real effort by a would-be author, a real effort was made by this reader to assess it.

When it becomes known that a man is a publisher's reader, his professional services will be in demand by many others besides his employer. Near relations, distant connections, old friends, new acquaintances, persons who have been recommended to approach him or are even quite unknown to him, and bores of every imaginable and of many a not easily imaginable kind will ask him to read what they have written and give them his advice. They do sometimes say, 'I realize how busy you are, but——' If these supplicants realize that they are picking the brain and soliciting the help of a professional man, they do not always show it, either by offering him a fee, making him a present, or even thanking him for bringing his innate and acquired expertness to bear. He cannot help addressing himself to every single new typescript at least with mild curiosity—which is only a very distant connection of hope. It is not nothing to find out what a human creature has chosen to commit to paper as his or her response to the opportunity of living and of exercising the body, the brain, the heart, and the imagination in this bizarre world. Even if the writer's motives are no stronger or more complex than vanity and a hope of gain, it must be at least of momentary interest to see what kind of utterance these motives have driven him to: it is more likely than not to be an utterance of mush.

As a pearl-diver may be presumed to prise open every dull and commonplace-looking oyster shell in case it has anything in it of the slightest value, so the reader turns over every title page: it is never impossible that his eyes may be caught by the seed-pearl lustre of a tiny talent. But, as he sits in his study knee-deep among the empty shells of disappointed expectation, it is one of his constant exercises to convey to literary aspirants—and to practised authors as well—news that is unwanted and unpalatable. Civility requires a certain restraint. He has been taken into their confidence, and even if to enter it has proved only a backward step into the inane, he cannot decently tell them that they know what they can do with their typescript. On the contrary, with what he believes to be tact, restraint, patience, and politeness, commingled, he will have to convey, ninety-nine times out of a hundred, that his correspondent is an incompetent amateur deluded by vanity and ignorance, whose dull understanding has miscarried, who has been wasting the time of more than one person, and who might be more usefully and indeed more gainfully employed with a spade or scrubbing brush than with a typewriter. His command of evasive euphemism becomes so facile that diplomatists could go to school with him. It is an acquired skill that merits greater rewards than he is ever likely to receive.

There is no great mystery about what kinds of typescripts his adivser will suggest to a publisher are ripe for refusal. They will be those which are hopelessly obscene or libellous; those which are out of keeping with this list; and those which are bad in one of the many ways in which badness is possible—insane, for example, dull, stale, thin, cheap, pretentious, dim, flashy, or mushy. The typescripts which the adviser is likely to commend to the

At Home

publisher's attention will probably be in one of the following categories:

  (i) books with literary merit of some kind and with good and immediate commercial prospects;
 (ii) books with literary merit and possible long-term commercial prospects;
(iii) books with literary merit and no prospects of sales;
(iv) books of topical interest or importance;
 (v) books that might have prospects if they were improved, reduced, or expanded.

It is not generally realized, outside publishers' offices, that a great deal has often to be done, before the typewritten word is fit to print, in the way of suggesting or making improvements, and correcting errors of fact, taste, or judgment, as well as of construction, proportion, style, syntax, grammar, or spelling.

I was once asked what I considered the main difference between male and female authors of fiction, biography, and so on. I could only reply that males tend to be too solemn and earnest, females too trivial and unselective. If women sometimes tend to regard everything that happens as of equal significance and to be unable to seize upon or evolve what is summary or symbolic, the seriousness of men can be doughy, doctrinaire, and deadly. Never impressed by undue earnestness, I have often and often been reminded of what Sydney Smith wrote to Bishop Blomfield, 'You must not think me necessarily foolish because I am facetious, nor will I consider you necessarily wise because you are grave.'

In its way, I believe, a varied experience of the typewritten word has been as valuable to me, in learning to understand human nature, as a good deal of the varied experience I have had in contact with living persons. I have certainly learnt something about the weaknesses as well as the virtues of authors and would-be authors, publishers, and publishers' advisers. If there is one conspicuous common attribute of authors it is the same one so much in evidence among human beings generally, I mean vanity. Evidently some degree of self-esteem is necessary if we are to get through life at all, but it does sometimes seem as if the act of darkening paper with rows of words also darkens the writer's ability to regard himself with detachment. The self-importance and touchiness of authors is no longer a surprise to me, nor is their capacity for envy and malice. But even graver, among would-be authors, is a general incompetence. It is disquieting to find how often people have nothing to say, and say it at length and badly.

One might think it the first business of a would-be author to try and reach some approximate assessment of what he is or is not able to do. He has before him frequent bad examples in print of the work of known authors who exhibit the same fault, and he has illustrious examples of all kinds from whom to learn; but the miseries and splendours of others are nothing to the self-absorbed; he will not try and form himself on good models, he will not perceive the dangers of bad ones; and self-doubt, like self-examination, is beyond him. Incompetence and stupidity have no bounds, and the self-absorbed would-be author often shows himself totally indifferent to the inclinations of any kind of reading public, so to whom he supposes he is addressing himself remains totally obscure. Still stranger is his bad presentation of what he is trying to sell. Every publisher knows those typescripts which are third or fourth carbon copies, sometimes done in single spacing with a worn-out typewriter ribbon; those dirty, dog's-eared typescripts, fouled with cocoa stains or cigarette ash, which have evidently been hawked about in vain; those long fictions clamped in some formidable binding cover, too heavy to hold with ease, and impossible to open flat; those spring-back covers from which the contents are apt to fly out, with all the élan of a kangaroo, the sheets when recovered proving to be unnumbered; those long productions typed on something like toilet paper and fastened imperfectly with sharp, stiletto-like fangs of brass not only apt but poised to cause a nasty wound. And all this has to be faced before attempting to investigate what is almost certain to prove yet another dreary hotch-potch of cliché, cant, and commonplace.

And what are the little weaknesses of publishers? They are those of the rest of mankind, with some occupational variations. They tend to be either too literary or too commercial. If they are too ready to publish work of some literary merit or potential promise and are at the same time short of experience, capital, flair, and commercial acumen, they may be, as publishers, benefactors of mankind but without staying power. If they are too disdainful of literary merit and too greedy for profit, and have no more than the faculties of businessmen, then they are nothing more than businessmen. Like other people, publishers may be too old-fashioned or too up to date: if they are advanced in years, they may fail to realize, like other old men, that the swans of yesterday may be dodos today; if they are young, they may think newness, fashionableness, and topicality of an enduring nature. And it is always interesting to notice that publishers, like other people, have their blind spots and little manias; like other people they reject chances of backing a right horse, and obstinately back wrong ones.

It will not be for a moment supposed that publishers' advisers are immune from all the failings of authors and would-be authors, publishers and might-have-been publishers. Vanity easily gets a hold on them. Long practice in discrimination easily tempts them to think themselves infallible, and the sheer drudgery of a perennial inspection of many varieties of tripe makes them liable to irritability. They too have their prejudices and passions, their blind spots and little manias. They are liable to advise the rejection of typescripts that might have popular success and be moneymakers, or success of esteem followed perhaps by durability and influence. Or they may advise the acceptance of typescripts that flatter or appeal to some personal quirk, interest, or enthusiasm of their own.

I have heard that Edward Garnett could not bear, let alone enjoy, the writings of Firbank. Not to perceive their technical innovation, skill, and influence seems to me a blind spot; not to be able to enjoy their wit and fantasy seems to me a sad deprivation. But then I have myself more blind spots than any leopard. I will not betray myself by displaying them in public, but I do not feel (to give a single instance) that there would be a general consciousness of a dreadful void in modern literature if there had never been any such writer as—but no, what is the good of flogging a dead dog? What seems to me certain is that the services of a man like Edward Garnett, or of a man like Daniel George in these later times, are so helpful that their little failings must be allowed for. That capricious and amorphous mass, the reading public, has in general little or no conception of the functions of a publisher's reader, and even literary persons are often strangely unaware of the great obligations not only of would-be authors, but of accepted and admired authors, to the careful thought, the patient coaching, and the laborious revisions that occupy much of the nights as well as the days of such men. Of what publishers owe them publishers ought to be the best judges.

The functions of a publisher's reader are far more complex than I have indicated. He has to act as a kind of barometer in relation to the literary weather. For example, any reader during the last forty years will have had something to do with war books. Whether after the First or the Second World War it was necessary to judge not only the merits and originality, but the timeliness of such books. It became sadly clear to those who saw them in an unpublished state that for many a male inhabitant of this country service in the armed forces in time of war had provided a one and only personal experience of any significance. This may be taken as an indication of the sobriety and security of English life in general, and also of the stimulating effect upon sober souls of danger, excitement, comradeship, violence, and suffering. But for a man to be driven to some fictional or reminiscent expression of the effect upon him of these stimuli, though it might in some instances result in a noteworthy book, seldom proved that the author of it was thereby equipped to follow it up and become a professional writer. And to the hard-working reader, in the years after the Second World War, it must often have seemed that almost every man who had been airborne, or at sea, or in the Eighth Army, or a prisoner of war, had felt impelled to write some sort of book about it.

Part of the publisher's adviser's task is to try and discern at what moment saturation point has been reached in regard to any form of book. And for this it is necessary for him to be au courant with changes in habits, taste, and education, and with the effects upon them of economic change and pressure. In the Thirties, for instance, a publisher's reader thought he could recognize pretty easily what would be considered obscene (even though he did not necessarily think it so himself), and he was able to warn the publisher accordingly. But after the Second World War, partly owing to a spread of candour under American influence, he could no longer be sure what would or would not be considered

obscene. Fiction, in particular, is seen by him to be peculiarly subject to changes of taste. It is said that before the War fiction made
up something like thirty per cent of the total of new books published in England, and that today it is less than twenty per cent,
while nearly three times as many technical books are published,
and nearly twice as many on art and architecture. In the Thirties
there were certainly a great many empty souls with leisure, who
filled their heads and their time with more or less trivial fiction.
Now leisure has diminished, tastes have changed because people
have changed and ways of life and thought have changed; novels
have changed because the writers of novels have changed; and,
also, the high costs of book production now make it far more of a
risk for the publisher to issue novels. Right up to the War there
was still a considerable concocting of regional and rustic novels.
Today there are only vestigial remains of regionalism and rus-
ticity, and England has become more like one large town with
standardized habits of life and thought. But to begin discussing
what is called 'the novel' is to risk spreading tedium, and this is
not the place to do it. My own belief is that, since the novel in the
nineteenth and twentieth century has been evidently not only one
of the highest and most elastic forms of literature, but one of the
most valuable means of interpreting social and private life, and
one of the most various and splendid forms of entertainment ever
evolved, there is no reason to stand around lecturing, or sit
around theorizing, whether orally or on paper, on the real or
imagined decline and supposed future of 'the novel'. So long as
ficiton is well written by new and resourceful authors it is likely
to find readers.

Although in the Thirties the examination of novels took up a
larger part of the time of an adviser to a general publisher than
perhaps it does today, it should not be thought that his attention

M

was not given to many other forms of writing—biographies, travel books, criticism, verse, and miscellanea. Not long after I had begun to read typescripts professionally I was asked if I had 'discovered any masterpieces'. Simple, romantic souls imagined that such a process was one of the rewards of this occupation. Luckily I was soon able to tell them that I had had to do with a book that seemed to me of exceptional interest and some importance. It was not a work of fiction.

13

The Curate of Clyro

THE word was not always typewritten. Short stories or experimental verse by some girl or boy might arrive in manuscript, a charwoman's memoirs, or some crazy dotard's demonstration, by means of numerology or cryptograms, that Bacon was the Dark Lady of the Sonnets. Also one was exposed to a desultory bombardment of matter written before typewriters were invented, and preserved by family pride. It was, and still is, a delusion widely held by persons who ought to know better that antiquity is in itself a virtue. Those eighteenth-century letters from a member of Parliament, that diary of a carriage tour kept by a young lady who visited the field of Waterloo in the 1820s, may serve, dear sir or madam, to inflate your over-estimate of your own forebears, but I do assure you that wigs, flowered waistcoats, and shoe buckles were often inseparable from pompous mediocrity, and that bonnet and shawl were no less often the ornaments of skittish inanity; and, further, that dullness is often hereditary. Ancestor worship, when examined, is sometimes found to be an inflation of nincompoops. To receive one morning from a man in Dorset a couple of old notebooks which he said were specimens of his uncle's diary was not in itself therefore to feel pressure on the trigger of expectation: it was only when I began to read them that the pressure was perceptible.

What I saw made me send for the rest of the diary. It was contained in twenty-two notebooks closely written, as if for economy, in a cramped, angular hand characteristic of the period, which was the mid-Victorian, and was the work of a country clergyman who had died before he was forty. Like most diaries it was largely trivial and of ephemeral significance, but unlike most diaries it was the work of a writer of character and sensibility. I believed that if it were winnowed it might be made into a book of more than ordinary interest and of some importance. I undertook to edit it myself, and the process took up much of my time for three years. Kilvert's Diary was published by Jonathan Cape in three volumes during the years 1938, 1939, and 1940, and soon became famous. If it had been published as it stood it would have filled nine stoutish volumes, running to well over a million words. Not one of those words went unweighed by me.

I do not think this unique manuscript could easily have fallen into more interested hands. A strong predilection for autobiography; an association in boyhood with the very part of the Welsh border country where Kilvert had flourished; an interest in the Victorian age; a particular interest in literary country clergymen of that age, men like Hawker of Morwenstow or Charles Turner, the brother of Tennyson; associations, by heredity and early environments, with the Church of England; a liking for landscape; the sense of character of which I am conscious, and the nature of my literary taste — all these things seemed to have prepared me for the task of extracting Kilvert from his diary. Kilvert speaks for himself, and I have done a little to speak for him in the introductions to the three volumes of the diary and elsewhere. Appreciations of him by Dr A. L. Rowse, V. S. Pritchett and others have appeared in print, and he is by now a known and established minor writer with a place in the history of English literature, so to say much about him here would be to

harp on an old string. Pluck it I will, however, to give some ink-
ling of his human, period, and literary significance.

Francis Kilvert (1840–79) believed that life was 'a curious and
wonderful thing' and that to be alive was 'a positive luxury': no
wonder he wished to record it. The result of his recording it is a
detailed picture of country life in the 1870s which is, so far as I
know, unmatchable. It is a perfect piece of social history, which
confirms what is known from other sources, contradicts what is
falsely assumed, and is the work of a rare and graphic artist. Kilvert had an eye for his surroundings and a command of words to
record the shape and colour of what he saw. 'His great virtue,' as
Humphry House wrote, 'is the power of conveying the physical
quality of everything he describes.' He accepts without question
the social stratification and conventions of his time, so he writes
naturally of social life. And he writes with a surprising frankness at
times about himself. His natural male appetites and expectancy
were constrained by his priestly status and sense of responsibility;
by a sense of sin; by social decorum; and by his celibate state,
which seems to have been protracted by want of money. But if his
appetites were repressed or sublimated, they did not disappear. He
continued highly susceptible to all feminine beauty, the younger
the better. As I wrote in the introduction to the second volume
of the *Diary*, Kilvert in his middle thirties was in a state of almost
continual bewitchment and emotional upheaval, tended to endow
natural phenomena with feminine personalities, and was at least
once on the brink of a major indiscretion. He does not hide any of
this. Some readers have found his supercharged rhapsodizings over
young girls mawkish, and his interest in flagellation morbid;
others have praised his candour. At least his feelings may have
helped him, as a priest, to understand and perhaps allow for the
little weaknesses of others. There was something magnetic about

him. An old cousin of his told me he remembered him as 'very sleek and glossy and gentle, rather like a nice Newfoundland dog'. Glossy sleekness, an envelope of well-being, might easily be attractive. Kilvert's nephew told me that he had 'a curious power of attracting', and Kilvert himself alludes to what he calls his 'strange and terrible gift' of exciting love. He eventually married, in his thirty-ninth year, and died suddenly just over a month later. His wife survived him for thirty years. It had been her hope to be buried beside him in Bredwardine churchyard, but she had delayed so long that the remains of two maiden ladies were already installed on either side of him, so she had to lie at a distance—a turn of events which seems made to have been the theme of a poem by Hardy.

While editing the diary I revisited what has now come to be known as the Kilvert country, attaching myself at once to local life by staying at a farm on a hillside above Kilvert's village of Clyro in Radnorshire. As soon as I got there I went out into the fields to help with the work. Every lane and path was identifiable in the *Diary*, which was already known locally. Reviewers had compared Kilvert to Dorothy Wordsworth, to Proust, to Pepys, to Amiel, to Gerard Manley Hopkins, and even to D. H. Lawrence, but round about Clyro persons were still living who could remember him and felt no need of such comparisons. I had seen him in his full-length manuscript diary as he appeared to me; I had seen how he appeared to various readers of the published *Diary*; and now I learnt what sort of fragrance his memory had left round about Clyro. There was Mrs Amey, for instance, who wrote to me from Cusop to tell me how men had waited in her mother's cottage at Bredwardine for Kilvert's return from his honeymoon, and how they took the two black horses out of the shafts and pulled the carriage to the vicarage through the pouring rain. Seventy years later Mrs Amey still cherished a photograph of Kilvert and his wife. They were people worth remembering, she said. She told me of his discretion: 'You could tell him everything and you knew it wouldn't go any further.' And she said that whenever he had a chicken for his dinner he always cut off a good helping before he began, and took this afterwards to some sick parishioner. With such anecdotes this Christian man was remembered and his memory cherished. After 70 years he seemed to be still living. *He being dead, yet speaketh* is the fitting inscription on his grave; his magnetism and his gift of exciting love gave him a kind of immortality, driving him, year after year, to build up by candlelight, phrase by phrase, his own monument. Against his window the colossal country silence pressed—like wadding, but not too thick to shut out the cry of an occasional owl or the sighing hiss of rain. Already the last decades of silence were passing; perhaps the hush was never deeper than then, before the pandemonium set in, of motor traffic, radio, aircraft, and bombs. In that doomed hush he lived and wrote.

One blazing midday, after a bathe in an ice-cold pool under a ferny waterfall, I made my way over rough ground to a house called Whitehall. In Kilvert's day it was in ruin, and he has left a Hardyesque account of it. A house with a past, it had been the scene of rough merrymakings after hard work long ago. Since his day it had been rebuilt and lived in and had again fallen into ruin. Under the vertical sun two owls in the ivy just above my head stared at me with amazement and incredulity. If I had been Kilvert himself—or Dr Gruber—they could not have been more surprised. Not far off were places that meant much to Kilvert and had changed little since his time, Whitty's Mill and Bettws. The unpopulous landscape, which emigrants spurred by enterprise and economic pressure had long been deserting for distant countries and other countries, retained its richness and wildness. A roadman in a lonely lane told me I might not admire this countryside so much if I had to get a living out of it. His world, the world of the lonelier hill-farmers, was no softer than that visioned later in the poetry of R. S. Thomas. It was a world of old ruralities, still a Kilvertian world, where it was possible to encounter a girl carrying homemade perry over the fields to some unmechanized haymakers, to gossip with a voluble blacksmith at his forge, to visit a recluse in a half-ruined house crammed with mouldy books. You can't live on a heath and be vulgar, said Hardy, and those who lived on this heath spoke with meaning and were hospitable to a stranger.

Sweating from one of many long walks, I sat on a bank of heather in the afternoon sun, listening to the seedpods of the gorse bursting open in the heat. Between me and the climbing flowery hills lay the Rhos Goch, a sinister bog where many have been drowned; over there was Llanshifr with its dark past, and Cefn-y-Blaen, where giants once lived; and there was the road to Newchurch, up which Kilvert, bearded and repressed and dressed in black, used to stride to see his sweet but *maladive* Emmeline; and further off was the beautifully named and remote Michaelchurch-on-Arrow, through which I had just been wandering myself. (So late as 1955 the church there had no lighting, and at the harvest festival service each member of the congregation brought with him a candlestick with a lighted candle in it — a scene that would have delighted Kilvert.) All very well in the summer, the hinterland of Radnorshire, but a smallholder up in the hills told me he always took a spade to bed with him in the winter; he never knew when he might wake to find his house snowed up and have to dig himself out. Only a couple of winters before, a young married woman with several children, the wife of a farmer away up in the hills, went down on horseback on Christmas Eve to Hay (just across the Wye from Clyro) to do some Christmas shopping. There was snow on the ground and in the afternoon a wild snowstorm set in. Friends tried to dissuade her from returning home, but off she went. She wanted the children to find their stockings full when they woke in the morning. In the dark blizzard she lost her way, and was found by a search party on Christmas morning, frozen to death, face down in a snowdrift, with the presents for the children clutched in her hand.

The region was still a region, not yet part of a standardized, suburbanized, industrialized England without secrets. Even after the Second World War it retained something of its former character. I remember hearing then of the two old brothers who lived together at the ruined cottage on Cusop Hill, beyond Trevannoc, on the northern slopes of the Black Mountains. They were reclusive and illiterate. One or the other used to come down once a week to Hay to draw their old age pensions. They signed with a cross. Once, when one of the brothers came down, and somebody asked how the other was, he said, 'I don't know what's the matter with him. He's been lying in bed these last two or three days and when I speak to him he won't answer me.' It was felt that the silent brother might be ill and in need of attention, so somebody went up to investigate. His silence was easily accounted for; he had been dead for some time. The place had fallen into decay when I was last there. Approached by a grass-grown avenue of stunted, wind-bent hawthorns, with rain driving across the lonely moor, it was an old-world image of desolation.

Kilvert was a frequent visitor to Hay, and especially to the Bevan family at Hay Castle. A more recent and more notorious local figure was more vividly remembered there. Hay had, as they say, 'become news' with the discovery that one of its respected citizens, a professional man who used to read the lessons in church, was a murderer. Through the sham-Gothic machicolations of the Jubilee Clock Tower crouching detectives watched him crossing from his office to the chemist's to buy arsenic 'for dandelions'. His first 'dandelion' was his wife, neatly done away with in their neat villa with its hanging wire baskets of geraniums and its ornamental ironwork painted dead white. A local friend of mine had had a drink with him one evening after he had already attempted to get rid of the second 'dandelion'.

'The trouble is,' he said, confidentially tapping my friend on the knee, while discussing this second victim, 'the man isn't a gentleman.'

It became known later that he had invited this dandelion to tea. 'Excuse fingers!' he had said gaily, as he pressed his guest to a carefully prepared arsenical scone-and-butter.

There is always plenty of scope in such a place for a Kilvert. The trouble is that good diarists are excessively rare.

An interesting consequence of the publication of *Kilvert's Diary* was the proposal to form a Kilvert Society. It came from the late Sid Wright, a merchant of Hereford. He was a man of unmistakable benevolence with a lifelong knowledge of the Border country and a keen interest in both the human and topographical aspects of the *Diary*. I was in favour of the proposal for a number of reasons, and in a lecture at Hereford appealed for support of it. Soon after the publication of the last volume of the *Diary* I had learnt that Kilvert's grave at Bredwardine was in a state of neglect, and had corresponded with his nephew about this. Fortunately a local admirer of the *Diary* had put it in repair, but I felt that a Kilvert Society might assume the responsibility for keeping it in order. Then I had had complaints from readers of the *Diary* who had gone on pilgrimage to Clyro and had searched in vain for some sign of Kilvert's having lived and served the Church there. I urged that whether there was to be a Kilvert Society or not, steps should be taken to put up a memorial tablet in the church at Clyro as soon as possible. I suggested that the best way to commemorate Kilvert was to read his *Diary*, and another way was to see that as far as possible the places he loved should be kept unspoilt by unsightly buildings or advertisements, or by invasions of trippers scattering litter. I argued in favour of promoting consciousness of local history and tradition, in both of which Kilvert could now be seen to occupy a significant place, and accordingly in favour of the collection of records and associations concerned with the diarist himself and with relevant persons and places. Naturally there were signs of a want of enthusiasm on the part of dunces, materialists, and sentimentalists. There were snobs or envious commercial rivals, who resented the leading part being played by Sid Wright. Illiterates, so far as they were capable of wonder, wondered what all the fuss was about. And the sentimentalist view had been put as early as 1939 by an amiable contributor to *Country Life*. He was like those persons who would fend off sightseers from Haworth and, if logical, from Stratford-on-Avon too. 'Some of us', he wrote, 'shudder' to see a charabanc labelled 'The Hardy Country' and so on:

> We feel there is something of desecration in a three-and-sixpenny tour of these districts. They are precious, almost faery regions, steeped in mystery and rich with treasure, to which, we rightly judge, the 'Open Sesame' costs rather more than three shillings and sixpence.

But even by heading his article 'The Kilvert Country' and dwelling on its 'enchantment' he was drawing attention to his precious, faery region. And why not? So far as I know, nothing but good has come of the Kilvert Society.

The inaugural meeting was held at Hereford in July, 1948, and preceded by a mayoral reception. The declared object of the Society was 'to foster an interest in the Rev. Francis Kilvert, his work, his *Diary*, and the countryside he loved'. A delightful coloured film was shown, after my lecture, of scenes in the Kilvert country, and on the next day a service of commemoration was held at Bredwardine church. The preacher was the Dean of Hereford (the Very Rev. Hedley Burrows), who had shown an early and keen interest in Kilvert, and had laid proper stress on his significance as a priest. The lessons were read by the Vicar of Clyro, the Rev. J. Lloyd, and J. P. L. Thomas, M.P. (now Lord Cilcennin), and before the service the Dean had dedicated in the churchyard a stone memorial seat with an inscription finely carved by Sid Wright, who had been unanimously elected first president of the Society. I wound up the proceedings with an oration in the village hall. In the following year a memorial plaque was duly unveiled in the church at Clyro, and every summer a service of commemoration has been held in one or other of the parishes associated with Kilvert. There have also been organized visits to various places round about, and to Kilvert's other country in Wiltshire. After Sid Wright's death, his widow succeeded him as president, and the Society is blessed with a most energetic and well-informed secretary, C. T. O. Prosser.

I give these few details to show how Kilvert's local fame has been upheld. I cannot believe that he would have been displeased to know that his homes and haunts have become places of pilgrimage, though he might have been surprised, because he seems to have been a modest man little aware of his uniqueness and of his literary power. He is, I suppose, now generally recognized as one

The Curate of Clyro

of the half-dozen best English diarists, and I am naturally pleased to have had so much to do with him. Perhaps some day some rich foundation may subsidize the publication of the diary in toto; it will then be possible to judge my abridgement of it, which I am pleased to say was approved by Kilvert's nephew, the owner of the manuscript. As my selectiveness was exercised with the general reader (that mythical creature) in mind, it would be found that I was not able to do full justice to Kilvert's preoccupation with his priestly functions. But, to judge from the utterances of the late Bishop of Swansea and Brecon and other dignitaries of the Church, I do not believe his repute as a faithful parish priest could be higher than it is.

I recall with pleasure the essay on *Kilvert's Diary* by V. S. Pritchett. He notes the diarist's sincerity, sensibility, and dignity; the acuteness of his eye and ear; his power of writing straight from nature; his lack of self-importance or self-consciousness; his art in conveying the chance effects of life, and his art in rendering tenderness of feeling—'an art which we have lost'. (Perhaps we have learnt to be ashamed of it; 'toughness' has been the common ideal in this century—and look where it has led us!) V. S. Pritchett sums up in these words:

> When we contrast the note and rhythm of our lives with those of Kilvert's, we see there is more than a change of fashions between the generations. We perceive with a shock that it is *we* who are unnatural, because we do not live within the walls of a long period of civilization and peace.

14

An Extra Skin

IN January, 1937, I happened to be living on the ground floor
of a house that overlooked the route taken by the funeral procession of King George V. Extract from a letter to my
parents:

I was awakened at early dawn by the buzzing of some thou-
sands of people outside the window. It reminded me of the
sound of the London crowds that Gissing heard on the Jubilee
Day in 1887 — 'the low, unvarying sound that suggested
some huge beast purring to itself in stupid contentment'. It
certainly didn't suggest mourning, but a mood of expectation. Between nine and one it would have been next to impossible to leave the house even if one had wanted to. Without asking permission, people even stood on my windowsill,
so I had to stand on the inner sill to see over the tops of their
heads. They smashed a balcony on the next house, and a large
slice of it is now hanging by a thread. They smashed branches
of trees in the square. And sometimes they went for each
other: some women on a sort of grandstand beat off with
their umbrellas some late arrivals who tried to climb up to
get a view — the sort of thing one might have seen, I suppose,
at a public execution a hundred years ago. 'Did you ever!'
said Mabel, bringing me some tea. 'They're just like a horde
of wild animals.'

An Extra Skin

Ten thousand people are said to have fainted, but this is no doubt a reporter's estimate, calculated to provoke more exclamations of 'Did you ever!' No doubt a great many more caught colds. It was an unattractive crowd, ugly, dowdy, and abounding in faces that wore stupid, cold, or vacant expressions. Apart from the people in front or those perched up high, few can have seen much of the procession. Many of the people at the back used cardboard periscopes, which mostly reflected a whole forest of other periscopes. It did not seem as if they were missing much. The procession was ill-organized and straggling; there were unaccountable delays, and dreary detachments of soldiers in khaki lent no splendour to the occasion. I saw some of the representatives from other countries chatting animatedly, shrugging their shoulders at a long hold-up, and exchanging jokes. The crowd chattered like monkeys the whole time, especially when they recognized personages whose faces they knew from newspapers and news films. The personages looked like their photographs, but not so clear. When the crowd dispersed, it left the usual vast excretion of litter.

In the afternoon I went to the Woolves, where I found Elizabeth Bowen and Iris Origo and Ethel Smyth . . . I went on to Elizabeth's to dinner, and Eliot was there. His gravity seemed decidedly male in comparison with those exceptionally quick-witted women with their shining eyes and brilliant, rapid utterance (in Iris Origo's case extremely rapid) outpaced by the quickness of their brains and senses.

There have been times in history when the death of a monarch has seemed to mark the end of an epoch, but on that day I seem to have been more impressed by the quick than the dead. I did not feel as I had felt when I heard of the murder of the Czar, which really did seem to mark an end. But epochs are not quite like plays, on which a curtain rises and falls: they overlap, they are untidy round the edges. Sometimes they are identified with dictators—'the Napoleonic era', 'the rise of Hitler', and so on. George V, born in 1865, was a Victorian, and the Victorian age seemed to be petering out at about the end of 1918. The British Empire seemed to end with the news of the fall of Singapore; the Thirties seemed to end with the fall of France in the summer of 1940; the Asia I had known, at Pearl Harbour. Eminent persons die; prodigious institutions begin to change or decay; cities are destroyed, countries invaded and occupied; but many individuals survive, and the relations between them and the public events of their time, infinitely variable, may be closer than they appear. As these pages are to some extent autobiographical, perhaps I had better look a little into my own relationship to the times about which I am writing. (It will be difficult, but there is the awful example of the elderly writer who said, 'Toute ma vie j'ai raturé, aussi mon œuvre est-elle nulle.')

On the surface it seemed a distant relationship; underneath it was closer than appeared. I am not a man of action, but a man of reflection. The more developed a man is, says Chekhov, the more he reflects, the more undecided he becomes, and the less inclined to take action. The action that had been taken between 1914 and 1918, the deliberate and elaborate slaughter of man by man, was quite enough to convert a reflective child to inaction for life, even if he had not been naturally inclined that way. Like any other reflective person, I guessed that another World War could not be long delayed. The Spanish Civil War was plainly a rehearsal for it, but I had not therefore felt impelled to learn how to kill other people or how to prevent them killing me. I believed that the springs of action, as Lowes Dickinson once said, lie deep in ignorance and madness. I wished to cultivate my understanding and to be sane. The dangers of such an intention are obvious. They may make a man feel superior, smug, priggish, and fill him with that intellectual vanity which is a form of spiritual pride, with the distasteful self-sufficiency of the rationalist. And they may unfit him for action when action—at least in the judgment of others—seems vital. If, of course, he were wholly detached and wholly pessimistic, he would have no fear of death or other consequences: but who is wholly detached or wholly pessimistic? Not the cultivated, not the sane.

Looking back, I think I had something in common with Axel Heyst, Conrad's leading character in *Victory*. Heyst was nomadic. He was very little interested in worldly success. Early influences had made him aloof and non-attached. It was not weakness of character, or vice, that had made *him* resolve to drift; it was conviction. He saw, or believed he saw, that action was bound to be harmful and to cause suffering to oneself and to others. He thought that by drifting and taking no action he could avoid causing or incurring suffering. But the unarmed man is armed, although he thinks he isn't. Heyst was still armed with disgust, because he retained standards of taste in human behaviour; in other words he was armed with a conscience and a heart.

In my case, weakness and vice may have contributed to a tendency to drift, but with me too to drift had become almost a philosophy, a conviction, a way of life. If only I were Dr Gruber, and if Dr Gruber were a doctor of the psyche as well as of the body, it may be that I could now be more precise about the state in which I then found myself. Some glandular imbalance, some chemical excess or deficiency in the blood, some deep lesion in the unconscious, might be retrospectively diagnosed by him. All I can

N   193

do is to impersonate him, and with amateurish tests, palpations, and analyses try and discover the workings, and perhaps the disorders, of a discarded, earlier self.

I did not for a time believe in freewill. I think it probable that Far Eastern influences in early manhood had contributed to my fatalism, or determinism. I simply could not understand how human beings, who have no choice in regard to entering this world, could be so arrogant as to suppose that, having entered it, they immediately or even gradually gain the power to choose how they shall or shall not act. 'But if I come to a fork in the road,' one of them might have said, 'I can take the left turning or the right, or neither, or stay where I am, or turn back.'

To which I would have replied, 'Whatever you do will be in accordance with your character, which is predetermined by causes either inside or outside yourself.' Evidently to hold such a belief would not stop a man drifting, but it would not necessarily make him inactive: whatever happened, or failed to happen, his behaviour would be in character. A man of action would be such because it was his nature: a reflective man might be driven to action — as Heyst was — and perhaps too late.

The menace of public catastrophe seemed too great to imagine. When it came it would, I supposed, destroy much in civilization that had not been easily won; and it would destroy human beings who had not been easily evolved and could not be replaced; and it was bound to weaken liberal and humane ideas and ways of life. Tidal waves of cant and propaganda, greater even than in the First World War, could be expected. They would swamp whole nations with self-delusion and drive them to mutual destruction. It would not have been senseless to regard the prospect with despair; it was easy to regard it with a kind of resigned disillusionment, more especially during phases of grave private trouble—as when, for example, one of the persons I have loved best, with one of the most balanced and compassionate understandings, twice, from altruistic motives, made unsuccessful attempts to commit suicide.

Nothing can be more commonplace than the process by which hopeful, youthful, or romantic sentiment gives way to resignation, scepticism, or cynicism. It is almost a physical process, like growing up. But I do not wish to give the impression of drifting along in a state of fatalistic gloom. I am a person of considerable energy and powers of enjoyment, and they had not gone into abeyance. I was not without hope, and had not lost the ability to be amused. But I found my amusement sometimes taking an unforeseen course.

In common with millions of others, I have lived through an apocalyptic half-century. It would be tedious to make a list of the happenings and inventions that have made it so, but it hardly seems an exaggeration to say that the world has changed more in the lifetime of my coevals than in any other previous historical period. Political or religious revolutions are nothing new; inventions like printing and photography altered the workings of the human mind and the manner of human life; but the revolutions and inventions of our time appear to have set loose new forces which have greater power for evil as well as good than any previously imagined. Also, though the idea of 'total' war is ancient and primitive and was the rule with savage tribes, it has been given a completely new scope by the savage tribes of the northern hemisphere (including ourselves) whom we were brought up to take pride in as the makers and spreaders of civilization. Add to these considerations the effect of quick communications, and the instantaneous and universal dissemination of cant and propaganda, together with the mechanizing and standardizing of life; and the effect of the ideas of Marx, Freud, Pavlov, and others; and it must follow that human nature (which, we were once taught, 'doesn't alter') is altering.

It seems probable that in the present century the nature of Western man may have been undergoing an ever spreading and accelerating process of change. With its astonishing resilience and adaptability mankind has unconsciously been trying to adapt itself to the new strains and stresses — physical and mental — which its own activities have brought into being. And among the manifestations of this process of readaptation are the prevalence of materialistic principles and practice, whether under Marxism or capitalism; a decline in individuality; and the erection of 'toughness' (always, in some degree, a necessity) into an ideal. Perhaps we are to expect a gradual atrophy of the capacity of Western man to be touched, to be moved to sympathy or pity or happiness, or even to love, in the way that many people used to be unashamedly touched or moved in former times. If that is so, it is worth looking for signs of the process in the individual, and considering whether it should be counteracted, and if so, by what means.

An inflammable sensibility may or may not be an advantage. Apathy or callousness can only be enemies of civilization. But between the man of feeling and the man of no feeling there is a far more numerous species — the man of middling feeling. Forced to find some defence or anaesthetic against the violent complexity and complex violence of the world in which he finds himself, he may have grown, without knowing it, an extra skin. If in fact such a change has come over mankind in the past half-century, perhaps one might try and trace it in an individual. The difficulty would be to distinguish between the usual hardening process of experience and maturity, and the hardening process of adaptation to the peculiar experience of living in the twentieth century. If I am to try and trace the distinction in myself I can attempt to do it in terms of poetry.

I am not a prolific poet, but since I began to write I have never found prose the only possible medium. To be longed for are the clarity, order, and moderation of prose; but they are not enough. Poetry seeks to attain a clarity of a different kind; it makes an order of its own, and does not make it out of moderation, but out of intensity, complexity, and seemingly indefinable sensations. They seem indefinable because they require unforeseen arrangements of words. These sensations make the poet acutely conscious both of his alienation from the rest of mankind and of his membership of mankind. Poetry is an attempt to fuse together the sense of difference and the sense of sameness. The greater the sense of difference, the less familiar and generally acceptable his mode of expression is likely to be, and the more acute his consciousness of himself as a poet. The greater the sense of sameness, the nearer will be his mode of expression to what is used or easily grasped by his actual or hoped-for readers.

I see myself, in regard to poetry, as a lone prospector, engaged in an intermittent but lifelong exploration of a particular territory, where drought prevails, vegetation is generally sparse, ghosts abound, and cataclysms occur, yet where there are paradisal places, offering more than promises of joy and peace. In the earliest stages of prospecting, my discoveries were slight and fragmentary. I found stones that resembled what others had found, or handfuls of dust and rubble in which, now and then, there was the gleam of something hopeful and unusual. Sometimes, with out-of-date equipment, I opened up a worked-out seam, believing that it was not worked out. Sometimes my gain was a handful of semi-precious stones, which came in for the admiration of others, but were not much in demand. Then there came a time, in a borderland country which had never been properly mapped, when I was able to stake out a claim to an area in which I found a particular interest. I had long had my eye on it, but now I began to work away in it, and found more than I had bargained for. There is something to be said for a mine of one's own, even if it is not very productive, and even if it does not produce quite the metal one might have expected.

I had from the first a tendency to write poetry in which a response to character, in its associations of time and place, led to occasional celebrations of it in ballad-like form, not untinged with irony. In the mid-Thirties I found this tendency becoming stronger. In a volume called *Visiting the Caves*, for example, published in 1936, there is a piece called 'Murder on the Downs'. When confronted with this, as soon as it had been completed, I felt a mingled surprise and uneasiness, as if I were being impersonated. Somebody else seemed to have written it, not the self with which I thought myself acquainted. Was I perhaps Doctor Gruber? And was Doctor Gruber perhaps a poet?

The poem is about an erotic murder committed in daylight, in fine weather, on the Sussex Downs. So far as I know, the crime, its perpetrator, and its victim are wholly imaginary. The mild, familiar aspect of the country is noted in strictly and even scornfully anti-Romantic terms. There is a non-religious note as well, inserted apparently to emphasize the absolute estrangement of these two persons from the traditional beliefs and values of their environment. There is also a fatalistic note: the victim of the crime, in her last words, declares, quite unprotestingly, that it is what she expected; and there is no room for doubt that such an end is what she half invited and half desired. The whole happening is treated with a light, mocking touch as if it was quite as ridiculous as horrible or tragic.

The process by which a poem is evolved may be slow, complex, and obscure, but I think I recognize in this ballad a hardening of sensibility that had set in unconsciously. And I think it was the recognition of it that had given me a shock. Perhaps in looking back I am reading too much into it, but the mood of the murderer and his victim seems to me the prevailing mood of the period. Compulsive violence unchecked by religious scruples or humaneness was matched with compulsive, unreasoning surrender: there was no effort to avert what seemed invited, desired, and inevitable. What I do not quite understand is the psychological significance of the mocking tone. Is it a mark of resignation and passiveness? I do not think so. I see it as a mark of defensive adaptation to a world in which too tender a sensibility would be either useless, or a handicap, or a danger — or all three. A few years earlier it would, I believe, have been impossible for me to dwell upon, or perhaps even to perceive, and certainly to be witty about any aspect of the murder of Mrs Fernandez. And as for the subject matter, I have no morbid interest in crimes of violence; I have no more interest in crime than anybody else whose curiosity about human behaviour is excited by newspaper reports. But it is a truism that poetry can reflect coming events — and the most momentous coming events were acts of violence.

During the next few years I published a number of ballads, or ballad-like poems which, when they appeared in book form, I described as satires. In a prefatory note I said:

These satires are concerned with points in human experience at which the terrifying coincides with the absurd, the monstrous with the commonplace. Such points are perhaps commoner in our time than usual, for we have seen horror and absurdity on an enormous scale.

One of them, for example, describes playfully an innocent wartime gathering in a vegetarian guest house. The party is broken up by blast from a flying bomb, which flings among them a singed fragment of a dismembered horse. The bitter humour of the incongruous is softened by playfulness. Other poems in the same batch throw details of private behaviour similarly into high relief against backgrounds of doom and actual or impending disaster. When these, together with some later and less ominous pieces, were collected into one volume for publication in America, I gave it the title *Borderline Ballads*, explaining that I was naturally drawn to a region near the indefinable frontiers between seriousness and irony, between the tragic and the vulgar, between mockery and sympathy, and between the past and the present. I have once or twice been reproached with 'cruelty' and a choice of sordid themes. No defence seems necessary. The themes brought themselves forward. In so far as they are what used to be called 'unpleasant' they reflect an age for which unpleasant would be a very mild term. And what seemed cruelty in the treatment of these themes can only have been evidence of that hardening process to which I have alluded. Call it detachment, call it objectiveness, call it the growing of an extra skin, but do not call it cruelty. That would imply a wish to give pain, or a pleasure in giving pain, where no more is being done than to offer instances of how men and women behave, or might easily behave, in or near our own lifetimes.

A sense of the past has prevented me from limiting the subject matter of these ballads to contemporary characters. As Conrad said, today is a scramble, tomorrow may never come, and it is the precious yesterday that can never be taken from us. I have from time to time been so kindled by some episode told in an out-of-date book of memoirs, it has so exactly caught the atmosphere of a period, the uniqueness of a situation, and the quiddity of one or more persons that I have isolated it for enjoyment. And a wish to communicate and enlarge enjoyment has been part of the motive that has, soon or late, transmuted it into a ballad. The memoirs of Tom Trollope, brother of the novelist, those of Mrs Hwfa Williams, and the exceedingly dull ones of the Hon. Lionel A. Tollemache are among those which have stimulated me in this way. The ballads have been written to be declaimed or, where more than one person is made articulate, to be performed. Intended as entertainments, they have been received with every appearance of attentiveness and amusement — but not without uneasiness. They are by-products of an uneasy time.

A final instance is a ballad called 'The Self-Made Blonde'. An unaccountable mating of two main and separate emotions set going the impulse of composition. One was caused by a detailed account of the consequences to dwellings and their inhabitants of the bursting of a huge dam; the other by an oral description of a deaf and dumb prostitute, combined with a memory of personal acquaintance with a deaf-mute. The peculiar chemistry of ballad making, working upon these conjoined elements, brought into being what seems to me a sensual and macabre fable of love, or at least of erotic satisfaction, destroyed by force majeure. 'The worse taste your ballads are in,' said an old friend, a woman, on hearing this one, 'the better they are.' I took that as a compliment. I have not wished, in writing poetry, to see words and images cool or rot in some petrifying or putrefying atmosphere of so-called 'good taste.'

15

Incorrigible Barbarism

MRS HAGWORTHY, in Osbert Sitwell's *Miracle on Sinai* (1933), gave it as her husband's opinion that 'before a war we should do all we can, while fully prepared for it, to prevent it: and that when it becomes inevitable—which, under these circumstances, it always does in time—we should be the first to enter, and should prosecute it with the utmost violence'. But in the opinion of Father Munnion, a character in the same book, 'It isn't war: it wasn't war! It's something quite different. It shouldn't be called *war* any longer . . . It's more like an earthquake . . . something with which no individual or group of individuals can grapple.'

Anyone who happens to have read elsewhere of what I called my innate pacifism may wonder how—if it was innate, and if it was pacifism—this individual was preparing to grapple with an earthquake. The same question was put by a neat-looking woman in a coat and skirt who rang my front door bell in London in the autumn of 1938.

'Good morning,' she said pleasantly, raising a notebook in a kind of salute. 'I'm from the Town Hall. I want to inquire what you will be doing in the event of an emergency.'

In the event of an emergency! Could anything be more English than this memorable phrase? Did the Town Hall hold classes of instruction in the use of litotes? My first reaction (no less English) was naturally to say 'What sauce! Why don't you and the Town

Hall mind your own business?' But in fact I said, 'Do you mean when the War begins?'

She winced at such bluntness.

'If this is a Gallup poll,' I said, 'you had better put down that I don't know.'

She murmured something about organizing evacuation, a word which had hitherto suggested castor oil, and as this did not seem a desideratum, I politely wished her a good day.

In the event of an emergency! What had given rise to such a phrase? Refinement? Wishful thinking? Hypocrisy? War was now a certainty. Was she, or was the Town Hall, accustomed to refer to the Emergency of 1914–18, the Boer Emergency, the Hundred Years' Emergency, the Second Punic Emergency, or the Emergency of Jenkins' Ear? Cry havoc, and let loose the dogs of emergency!

How was one to 'grapple'? There was reason to suppose that the impending 'total' War would be catastrophic. There was no reason to be ashamed of feelings of disgust, disappointment, and depression. One might easily have said of the War what Gosse said to Gide about the publication of his *Corydon*, 'Is it wise? Is it useful? Is it necessary?' But if it was not to be called *war* any longer, what likelihood was there of any prospect of a later condition describable as *peace*? I had no firm belief in non-resistance as a principle, and at the same time felt no urge to fit myself for any precise part in what seemed as incalculable as an earthquake. But the possibility that the life of Europe might be dominated by an odious paranoiac like Hitler was clearly not compatible with civilization, and against such a possibility disapproval would not by itself be much of a defence.

To disclaim any concern with the War would have been ridiculous; to renounce involvement in it would have been impossible. Not even Axel Heyst would have been able to do that, nor would he have wanted to. The War was expected to be total. Apart, therefore, from any question of defence against attack, it was plain that everybody was in danger. It is a commonplace that danger can bring people together, and although it may be only the herd instinct that arouses a sense of solidarity, I found myself, as the danger approached, looking at those who are called ordinary people with new eyes. Often in the Thirties it had been easy to feel a dislike for that vulgarity which is 'the behaviour of other people' and for their foolishness or unseemliness. But now their humanness seemed to shine even out of ugly, cramped, mean, de-based urban types. It was not their unattractiveness that was con-spicuous now, but their vitality, innocence, and vulnerability. It was possible to see, as if in a light of revelation, what is meant by the saying that we are all members of one another. A protective feeling arose, a wish to help to spare 'ordinary people' from the consequences of their own impercipience.

It was all very well for Flaubert to complain, as he under-standably did in 1870, of the incorrigible barbarism of the human race and of the mystical element in war that enraptures the mob. But in 1939 it was as difficult to feel superior to the mass of man-kind as it was impossible to remain aloof from it. And it would have been a great mistake to suppose that it was only men of re-flection who were disgusted by the prospect and the event: I read lately that in October, 1940, Lord Alanbrooke had written in his diary, 'There are times when the madness and the fallacy of war almost choke one.' They did choke many.

This reminded me that as a child I was troubled by the paradox that professional soldiers, though trained to kill their own species, did not seem at all like murderers. Officers of the old regular pre-1914 Army, whom I had encountered because they were relations, or were acquaintances of my family or their friends, had often seemed (as some survivors still seem) amiable and balanced beings. Personable, alert, athletic, and moulded by tradition and discipline, they had excellent manners, unforced kindliness, and often a sort of boyish zest. They seemed to enjoy life and to be considerate of others. Some, the most obviously modest, had proved themselves brave. They compared more than favourably with many civilian types who had enjoyed freedom without responsibility, and whose weaknesses were not hidden from a child—self-importance, for example, cockiness, pompousness, sloppiness, mean-mindedness. Conventional yet genial, they tended to match the image of Uncle Durham. One liked and respected them, and without effort some of them might easily inspire, or had inspired, devotion. How was it, then, that their business was to slaughter their kind? Why did they seem more warm-hearted, courageous, and admirable than many civilians with, presumably, more idealistic principles? The paradox did not resolve itself. And as I grew older it was seen in relation to the paradoxical nature of Christianity.

The folly, and the economic folly, of war have never been more unanswerably commented upon than by two old countrymen in Devonshire during the First World War. What they said was recorded by Cecil Torr in his well-written *Small Talk at Wreyland*. 'What be the sense of their contendin'?' said the first. 'Why, us in Lustleigh don't wage war on they in Bovey, and wherefore should the nations fight?' The other man said, 'It be a terrible thing, this war: proper terrible it be. I never knowed bacon such a price.' One of them was offended in his reasonableness, the other in his pocket: but Flaubert's reference to the incorrigible barbarism of the human race suggests a concern with something more than folly; it is more like a willingness to admit something like the doctrine of original sin. He seems to imply the need of redemption.

Rationalists, philosophical anarchists, and other idealists some-times argue, or seem to assume, that man is naturally good but is corrupted by his own institutions, by tyrants, governments, bureaucracies, priestcraft, vested interests, property owners, and so on; and that he can put things right if he will only use his head and be unselfish. That man is corruptible is obvious; they imply that he is self-corrupting, and that he needs saving from himself, from the horrible conditions into which he continually gets him-self and his fellow creatures. But to expect his own good sense or goodwill to save him is fanciful. An occasional or fortuitous altruism, a well-intentioned inclination to mind other people's business, may be survivals of religion; they are not an adequate substitute for it. Where is man to look for hope except in faith in some power greater and less earthbound than himself? But if he looks to Christianity to deliver him from the madness and incorrigible barbarism of war the prospect does not seem good.

The paradox of Christianity is that while appearing to advocate peace it is militant, and often militarist as well. During the First World War it was a shock to many simple people, who had been taught that Christ was the Prince of Peace, and that we were to forgive those that trespass against us, and that peacemakers were blessed, to see, for example, priests publicly blessing instruments of destruction. Arguments are adduced to prove that Christ was not on the side of peace. The Thirty-Seventh Article laid down that it was lawful for Christian men to 'serve in the wars'. A good Christian, it is explained, cannot be a pacifist, because it is his duty to fight against evil. But men do not seem to be reliable judges of good and evil: the help of the same God is invoked by opposed nations, each believing that it has right on its side against a wicked enemy. Christians who might hesitate to join in a direct, calculated, warlike attack upon some other nation or faction than their own would still conceive that they had the right to join in the defence of their own nation or faction, and of their lives, families, and property. Not to defend oneself would be to lay oneself and one's children open to oppression, slavery, or extermination. But here paradox comes in again. If a Christian's hopes are properly fixed upon a future life beyond the grave, he ought not to shrink from suffering and martyrdom on this side of it. But such an attitude requires a degree of saintliness that would seem absurd to most men, and is far beyond their reach. Finding themselves attacked, or believing themselves in danger of attack, they naturally set about defending themselves, determined to maintain their own being or at least their property and 'way of life' for their own offspring or successors. Regardless of Lustleigh's reasons for aggression, Bovey springs to the defence: blood flows, and up goes the price of bacon. Paradox again arises in the act of defence: there is no exact division between defence and attack, and attack may be the best form of defence. Directly armed conflict begins (and often without it) the way is open for incorrigible barbarism.

There is nothing new, I repeat, in the *idea* of total warfare. Such warfare was habitual with savage tribes who did not exclude non-combatants, the weak, the helpless, the young and the old from their ferocity. Only the *methods* of Auschwitz and Hiroshima are new. Scientific ingenuity diabolically applied, monstrous extravagance and wastefulness, have made what was always cruel and unreasonable suicidal. Some years ago, two fine stags were found drowned in the lake in Arundel Park. They had been fighting, had become inextricably locked together by the antlers, and had fallen together, exhausted and inseparable, into the water. Their mutual murder was in fact a double suicide: each probably thought it was rightly defending its way of life; both perhaps invoked the help of the same antlered god against a wicked enemy.

Religion, it might be thought, is chiefly concerned with the private soul and its relationship with God, but it has been and often is constituted as something more like a claim upon God for the predominance of a particular race or nation. This is less unreasonable than it may seem. The soul can only attempt to commune with God by maintaining its own life and character; the nation fears that without Divine help it may lose its own life and character, and this fear is kept alive both by those whose political or economic power depends on its maintenance and by those whose spiritual power is derived from faith, or professed faith, and enabled by authority to function. But as history shows that religions which claim universal validity are open to abuses that may lead to corruption, injustice, and oppression, it is hardly surprising that nationalistic religions lead to similar abuses, and attempt similar justifications.

The less admirable consequences or accompaniments of Shintoism in Japan, for example, of Greek Orthodoxy in Cyprus, or of the Dutch Reformed Church in South Africa, are plain, but it would be indecent to condemn them without inquiry whether the Church of England is above reproach. From a national tradition a Church may derive its character and its strength to continue in existence, but whenever it allows itself to defer to a narrow and exclusive racialism or nationalism, or to support violence or falsehood, or oppression, or militarism, or persecution, in the name of justice or patriotism, or of law and order, it is bound to weaken the confidence of others in its claims, or even to destroy that confidence. All human institutions are open to abuses, but one does not therefore give up one's attachment to them or belief in them. When they are constituted for the service of God, it is even more important to hold fast to what is best in them. The beauty of the Church of England is partly in its Englishness—as that of Shintoism is in its Japaneseness, or of Orthodoxy in its Greekness, or of the Reformed Church in its South African Dutchness—but the greater beauties of these and other cults are not divided from one another by racial or national barriers; they belong to that exalted sphere where local virtue is a part of universal life and truth, or contributes to them.

If in fact man needs to look to some greater power than himself to sustain him and deliver him from evil, he must not expect to be able to rely solely upon ideas that seem to him reasonable. In one of Landor's *Imaginary Conversations* the view is expressed that 'religions keep and are relished in proportion as they are salted with absurdity', and that 'all of them must have one great crystal of it for the centre'. The elements of Christian doctrine—the Incarnation, for instance, the Resurrection, and the Ascension—must seem absurd to a rationalist, and may seem so to a moralist. There is an interesting passage in a letter written by Conrad (a moralist, if ever there was one) to Edward Garnett in February, 1914. He was ready to concede that Christianity was great and compassionate, and that it could be improving and softening, but he was irritated by its having arisen from what he called an 'absurd oriental fable'. It is questionable whether human beings are to be trusted as judges of what is or is not absurd. (An uncommonly strong impression was made upon me in the Thirties by a film of the documentary variety, which showed what are called ordinary people going about on an ordinary day, and had been taken without their knowing: the self-importance, purposefulness, lack of purpose, and incidental antics of the man or woman in the street, or the house, were absurdity's own self.) If Conrad meant the word 'oriental' to be understood in a pejorative sense, that was absurd of him. And the same is true of the word 'fable', since some of the profoundest utterances of humanity are in the form of fables. But when he went on to say that Christianity had very easily lent itself to 'cruel distortion', that it had 'impossible standards', and had brought 'an infinity of anguish to innumerable souls — on this earth', he cannot be refuted.

If Christianity is to be believed in, it cannot rely on its rationality or much of its record. Christianity is an aspiration. It can be believed as a poem can be believed, because of its language and imagery, and for what they offer, promise, and suggest. They offer hope, a view of life, and a way of life; they promise a compensation for evil and for suffering; they suggest what humanity is sometimes capable of. That it has given scope to weakness and wickedness is not the fault of Christianity but of those who have professed it. Not only is it used by evil as a pretext and a mask, but by mediocrity as a refuge. The Sacraments are effectual, says the Twenty-Sixth Article, 'although they be ministered by evil men': it might have added 'or ineffectual men'. But those who speak of 'empty churches' have seldom looked inside to see how full the churches are, and where churches are not full it is they themselves who have left places vacant.

'In my view,' wrote Canon Vidler of King's College, Cambridge, in a letter to *The Times* in May, 1957, 'both the clergy and the laity of the Church of England are, with rare exceptions, monstrously conventional and depressingly docile.' Exactly: it is easier to conform to a set of rules than to transcend them creatively. It is less disturbing to fall in with accepted, current, and prevalent social and political ideas and habits and to pretend that they are not in conflict with the basic tenets of Christianity, than to point out that they are (which is usually true) and act accordingly. Initiative is always dangerous; dogma and discipline can always be made an excuse for shirking or condemning it. But dogma and discipline are not the chief glories of the Church of England.

To claim that the Church of England is the only admissible form of Christianity would be as narrow as to deny the merits of other than Christian forms of religion. But it is a cult with a peculiar appropriateness to a civilized disposition. There is wisdom and beauty in its function as a *via media* between sectarianism and authoritarian rigidity and pretension. Among its peculiar dangers are the monotonous conventionality and depressing docility singled out by Dr Vidler. It is also, by its very tradition, in danger of conforming too narrowly with nationalist, and even militarist, forms and tendencies. And with what are those impossible standards of which Conrad spoke to be identified if not with puritanical disregard of man's physical needs and appetites? It is just as much a fault of Catholicism as of Protestantism to turn the sense of joy to a sense of guilt, and unless Christianity can teach that cruelty is more obscene than sexuality, and that the idea of praise is more fruitful than the idea of sin, it will not deserve the support it ought to deserve.

A writer, an English writer, may exist snugly enough in the shelter of agnostic indifference, or drift easily along on the dirty current of materialism, preening himself from time to time on his superior wisdom. But if he has any sense of the literature which he pretends to be enlarging, or of the rich variety of literary character, genius, and talent associated with the Church of England since

the Reformation, let him ask himself whether, if he were to disregard it or its influence upon himself, he might not be risking
literary as well as moral bankruptcy. A Church which has been
found worth the support and adherence of Donne and Eliot, of
Jeremy Taylor and Sydney Smith, of Robert Herrick and John
Betjeman, is not to be written off as an outmoded fantasy because today it does not command, any more than before, the
support of youthful rebels, worldly wise busybodies, or fashionable entertainers.

It was the wise opinion of Jeremy Taylor that 'musick was
brought into Churches, and ornaments, and perfumes, and comely
garments, and solemnities, and decent ceremonies, that the busie
and less discerning fancy being bribed with its proper objects may
be instrumental to a more coelestial and spiritual love'. But
whether services be traditionally adorned or evangelically plain,
they cannot always be attended even by those who would wish to
attend them. The exercise and expansion of Anglicanism in the
nineteenth century may be variously accounted for; they could
not have occurred unless the educated classes had had the leisure
allowed by their ability to employ cheap labour in their homes.
Today, when so many of their descendants look after themselves
and find it a whole-time occupation, to go regularly to church, or
to go at all, has become scarcely possible. To look after themselves and their habitations and their children does not easily
allow them to look after their souls. The proper exercise of religion is thought to require communal worship and private
prayer. It also requires faith of some kind—which is often lacking
—and a degree of determinaton and persistence which are more
likely to be attainable by the old and retired than the young and
active.

In these conditions, it seems a pity that the habit of prayer is not more often and far more intelligently made acceptable to the young, so that when they are grown up they can heal and strengthen themselves and others by this exercise. Reason alone is too fallible. 'A boxe of Quicksilver,' said Jeremy Taylor: 'It looks to me otherwise than to you who doe not stand in the same light that I doe.' It is difficult to see how, unless prayer is added to meditation, an adequate power of self-criticism can be developed. Reason can always be used to try and justify selfishness, envy, self-pity, revengefulness, violence, war, and the opposites of what St Paul called 'love, joy, peace, longsuffering, gentleness, goodness, faith, meekness, temperance'. So can Christianity; but prayer can even show ways to overcome or avoid the abuses of religion and the harm done by the do-gooder as well as by the do-harmer. The only defence against the incorrigible barbarism of the human race (which lurks, is rampant, or is liable at any moment to re-appear in the human heart) is to attack it. Reason is a powerful means of attack, but it did not prevent the First World War; nor was it able to prevent, even after such unthinkable horror, the Second. Nor was religion. Neither was active enough, nor was there any proper liaison between them.

The road to hell may be paved with good intentions, but there are many worse pavements; and one need not be ashamed to be a product of a tradition of well-meaning. Where my own behaviour seems (though I can hardly judge it) to have been perhaps not wholly reprehensible, and where I have felt any strength to deal with difficulties, I have often felt indebted to my forebears. In the last couple of centuries they have often shown Whig, or liberal, or humane, or evangelical tendencies; the Church of England gave them form, method, and guidance; and who am I to contemn either the tendencies or the institution? What was good enough for our predecessors can never be good enough for us, because we live in different conditions and are different people. It is, or should be, part of the strength and wisdom of the English tradition, and of Anglicanism, that it can enlarge and adapt itself to changing circumstances. Otherwise the pleasure of being English would soon be only a memory.

16

His Light Still Burning

DURING the war I spent five and a half years doing what I thought fitted to do in that state to which it had pleased the Admiralty to call me. My situation was as characteristically anomalous as some of those earlier ones I have indicated in *Double Lives*. In plain clothes among uniforms, a harmless drudge among men of action, I was politely designated as a contradiction in terms, a 'civilian officer' on the Naval Staff. As a fish out of water, I was in my element. Allergic to seafaring ever since those childhood voyages back and forth between Southampton and the Cape, I detested the confinement, the motion, and the very smell of all ships. Fortunately those departments of the Admiralty in which I was confined were not afloat; they might sometimes have been pleasanter if they had been. The early attacks from the air were noticeable enough for a naval officer to be heard saying playfully to another, 'What! Going to sea, are you? So you're showing the white feather!'

London suffered much less than a number of other European cities, and I will keep my bomb stories to myself, except to say that I made the acquaintance of more than one 'near miss'—which term I translated, for the benefit of a Free French acquaintance, as *demi-vierge*. During the War years the senseless noise at night and the senseless destruction, the tedium of suspense and the repulsiveness of the news, were made up for by being often in agreeable company and making new friends and acquaintances.

At Home

In the later stages of the War, and as a result of it, I was ill with a hyperthyroid condition. The symptoms were disquieting. With the fine frenzy of an exophthalmic gleam intensifying behind the spectacles, a pronounced tremor, and disordered skin, digestion, and blood pressure, I was chiefly conscious of the workings of the heart, which felt and sounded like the engine of a motor bicycle. I felt myself rapidly receding from the vale of health. I was no longer, as they say, myself. Nor was I Dr Gruber, who would have taken steps to prevent the onset of such an affliction.

Life became distorted. Reactions to small stimuli were disproportionate. A sudden noise would produce an uncontrollable fit of trembling. A cup of coffee or a few pages of Balzac shook me to the roots of my being and seemed to fill the brain with blue sparks. Acutely pleasurable excitement alternated with its opposite, and a natural irritability began to verge upon mania, as if the body itself had developed a neurosis, from which the mind was not nearly as detached as it was accustomed to be. All this was disturbing to me, and must have taxed the forbearance of those who were either near or dear to me, or both. Harley Street insisted upon rest, but a sense of obligation was against it. After all (I was still able to reason), if at such a time everybody with a disordered metabolism took to bed, it would never do. I knew other people who had not allowed graver illness to stop them from doing what they had set themselves to do. I was not wounded or mutilated, or in any but a figurative sense a prisoner of war, so who was I to abdicate? Good advice, good medicine, a good constitution, and good luck united to display the team spirit, and gradually pulled me back from the troubled sphere into which I had felt myself inexorably drawn.

The atmosphere in November, 1918, had been exultant; at the end of the Second World War the temper of London seemed to be one of guarded relief. Furnished by naval authority with un-solicited testimonials, I found myself again living in Bayswater, a quarter on which I thought myself something of an authority. I could have pointed out the Red House, designed in 1874 by J. J. Stevenson, a friend of William Morris, and regarded by historians of architecture as a pioneer act in the revolt against the mid-Victorian conventions of house building; or the smallest house in London, which filled an interstice next to the Tyburn Convent, and of which the upper room measured thirty feet by four; or Nos. 23 and 24 Leinster Terrace, houses which were nothing more than façades masking an exposed section of the Metropolitan Railway.

I had already lived long enough to be well aware of change. The typical Bayswater house dated from the eighteen-fifties or eighteen-sixties. It formed one of a row of identical houses all joined together and designed by a speculative builder for the occupation of well-to-do families of the commercial, professional, or leisured classes. It consisted of a basement with a railed-in area, a ground floor, and four storeys above that. The front door was approached by two or three steps and overshadowed by a portico which supported a balustraded balcony. On the first floor there was a big double drawing room with an imposing chimney-piece of Italian marble, a decorated plaster ceiling, and french windows opening on to the balcony. The top floor consisted of attics originally intended as servants' bedrooms. The house was heated by open coal fires and lighted by gas, and the architects apparently took for granted the continuance, 'far as human eye could see' (never very far), of a standard of living immune to social, economic, and domestic changes of any magnitude. Not many years after the quarter was at its apogee it became necessary to adapt or convert many of the houses to modes of living much less lavish than that of the large and well endowed mid-Victorian family with its abundance of cheap coal, cheap servants, and elaborate meals.

In 1927 a topographer had written that 'the large houses of Bayswater have gone out of fashion as the homes of the wealthy classes and have been converted into maisonettes and private hotels'. Long before that, many of them had been turned into flats or boarding houses or apartment houses, or had lapsed into tenements or rookeries. While in 1870 Lancaster Gate was stylish enough for Cora Pearl to be kept in, and in 1906 was still stylish enough for Mrs Craigie to die in, the periphery of Bayswater, never smart, soon turned shabby or slummy. Even in the eighteen-eighties, streets and houses regarded as 'highly respectable' when new, only twenty years earlier, were already decaying. An example was the melancholy establishment in St Luke's Road, near Westbourne Park station, where W. H. Hudson, that rare migrant from the Argentine pampas, was for many years caged in by poverty, habit, and ill-health.

Even in some of the more pretentious streets many of those first floor drawing rooms had been divided up, between the wars, into bed-sitting rooms, sometimes euphemistically called 'one-room flatlets' or, later, 'divan-lounge-dinettes'. Many a business girl found herself living in a cell of inordinate height, with only half of an ornate plaster medallion in high relief on her ceiling, and only a thin partition between her and the occupant of the adjoining cell. A cold draught nipped her ankles when she climbed a gloomy flight of stairs to a conservatory converted into a bathroom, where she risked asphyxiation from the geyser, of which the chimney seemed, like the trunk of a pushing palm tree, to have forced its way through the glass into the open air. Often the task of adapting these houses to newer purposes and habits had seemed so daunting or futile that they had been pulled down and replaced by new blocks of flats, often with modern inconveniences of their own — like want of peace, space, and privacy — but more easily kept warm and clean. Or one could see, as in Stanhope Street (where my father was born in 1870), squat, 'easily run' houses of the Thirties adjoining Victorian houses of the old type.

In the eighteen-eighties, when my father was a boy, Bayswater was facetiously known as 'Asia Minor', because, like Bath and Cheltenham, it swarmed with retired Anglo-Indian soldiers and civil servants and their families. A number of cramming establishments were kept busy preparing the offspring to follow their fathers to India, and the shops in Westbourne Grove ('the Chowringhee of Bayswater' as a local chronicler called it) had good stocks of chutney and curry powder for the veterans in retirement, and of chlorodyne and cummerbunds for the departing tyros. Sixty years had gone, and in the later Forties the provision shops of Bayswater were expected to stock paprika, matzos, Knackwurst, and Schweinsohren. Since the rise of Hitler the population, both floating and settled, had become less and less English. Bayswater had for some time been favoured by the Jews and the Greeks as a quarter to live in, and by second class tourists as one to stay in: after the War it became steadily more cosmopolitan. In the frowstier 'guest houses' or 'private hotels' (which were neither private nor hotels), and in new and inferior restaurants, Irish waitresses or Cypriot waiters could now be seen planking down plates of so-called 'shepherd's pie' (which had nothing to do with shepherds and was not a pie), made of minced whale and a sloshy paste of water and potato powder, before some seedy cabal of ageing Baltic irredentists or the discarded mistress of a currency manipulator who had escaped from the debacle on the last tram out of Bratislava. Less than most waiters and waitresses did they know whom they might be waiting upon next — swarthy students of law, medicine, or the economics of immoral earnings, from Gambia, Trinidad, or Ceylon; or perhaps some Australian remittance girl with vain hopes of the concert platform and occasional walking-on parts in amateur documentary films, hesitating meanwhile whether to bestow her temporary and lack-adaisical favours upon a ruined Polish veterinary surgeon or a Hungarian publisher's nark. Such were some of the types who had largely ousted what was left of the indigenous bloc of well-to-do or depressed persons who with more or less reason regarded themselves, or wished to be regarded, as 'gentlefolk' — senescent, churchgoing ex-officers of the regular or the Indian army; theo-sophical widows and anti-vivisectionist spinsters, towed along by overfed, sex-starved, and incontinent dogs; survivals, misfits, or just 'ordinary' families or wage earners; so that now, if any survivors of this earlier population happened to hear the King's English spoken in the street, they looked up in amazement from their reveries, as if they were in Batum or in Bogotá.

Just as the edges of Bayswater — and not only the edges — had frayed into slums, so the population had a grubby fringe, or rather a fluid margin in which sank or swam the small-time spiv, the deserter, the failed commercial artist turned receiver, the tubercular middle-aged harlot, the lost homosexual, or the sex maniac. In the eighteen-fifties the Frith family, living at 10 Pembridge Villas, had been agitated by the real or rumoured activities of garrotters in the slums of Notting Hill; in the nineteen-forties Pembridgia itself knew crimes of passion, and one of its typically discreet-looking small hotels became a cynosure when it was reported to have sheltered the baleful energies of a quickly notorious erotomaniac murderer. I believe the gutter Press coined the term 'the Murder Mile' for the region just north of Notting Hill Gate. Occasionally I found myself passing the house which had once filled Mrs Fernandez with hope and her husband with suspicion, and I thought of old, unhappy, and already far off things.

The five and a half War years seemed like a slice cut out of my life, but what was the loss of a slice? To be alive, when so many others were dead, seemed a kind of privilege. To have survived two World Wars and a good many other hazards besides those of the Murder Mile, might cause a pious man to suppose himself spared for some special purpose, as if God were to say, 'You have been granted an extension of your lease of life. See that you make the most of it.' But it is not necessary for a man in his forties to be pious to begin to notice that his own light is still burning after other lights have gone out. He may become conscious more often than before of the briefness of life and may find himself a little more concerned not to waste it by surrendering to undesired pressures and fatuous intercourse: he may (if I may borrow an image from an unaccountably popular game) know better which balls to play.

'Do give me a ring,' a smart young woman said to me in such a dulcet voice that she seemed to be saying 'I am the honeysuckle, you are the bee.'

'Impossible,' I said, and explained that I disliked the telephone and its untimely intrusions.

'Oh, but you can't *not* have a telephone!' Her voice had turned shrill.

'Oh, *can't* I!'

One need not be a Cézanne to have as great a dread as his of *grappins*: and, as Alain Fournier wrote in one of his letters, 'Surtout il faut fuir ceux qui se prétendent vos amis, c'est à dire prétendent vous connaître et vous explorent brutalement.' Even by not cultivating quite pleasant acquaintances one is apt to be written off as an eccentric recluse, but that is a small price to pay for a modicum of solitude. Not, I hasten to say, that I was living alone, or living aloof. A man cannot expect to reach maturity without having acquired responsibilities for the welfare of others. He may be led to assume them by love or duty, or a mixture of both. The nearness of the last twenty years or so would make it untimely or unseemly to speak of my own more private responsibilities, even if I had a mind to do so, and I do not wish now to anticipate later happenings.

With my headquarters in the familiar but changed and changing environment of Bayswater, I began to address myself to a new phase of existence. I resumed my profession as a publisher's adviser, and had now begun to do a good deal of broadcasting, under the persuasion and tuition of John Morris. He had surprisingly returned from Japan in the middle of the war. I had not previously met him. We were drawn together by the fact that for each of us living in Japan had been an important and delightful experience, and before long we were all but blown to glory together by the same flying bomb. A solid and unemotional-looking man, a kinsman of William Morris, he had developed an Asian look, the protective mimicry that unconsciously moulds the facial expression, and almost the bones, of some Europeans who live, in a sympathetic frame of mind, among Asians in Asia. Years in a Gurkha regiment, a sojourn among the Lepchas, travels in Himalayan solitudes, a partial ascent of Everest, and a contented participation in the confidences and amusements of the Japanese, had arched the eyebrows above the spectacles, behind which the eyes were watchful rather than expressive; and the mouth, especially in uncongenial company, could be as immobile as the beak of the reputedly wise old owl who sat in an oak.

His Light Still Burning

Appointed to take charge of broadcasts to Asia, he invited me to take part in them. I had when young in Tokyo had some practice in trying to make English prose and verse, and English ideas, intelligible and interesting to Japanese ears; I now had to do the same for imaginary ears in Asia generally. I was assured that they existed, and were attentive. Improbable as this seemed, I found the writing and delivery of these talks a valuable exercise in composition and speaking; and when I spoke sometimes on the Home or the Third Programme (of which John Morris was later appointed Controller), it was no less valuable to learn to vary the content, diction, and tempo accordingly. The spoken word cannot oust the written word, but the ease with which it can now be transmitted or recorded is important for the writer. It is to be hoped that the spoken word will be raised to the level of the written word, and that the written word will gain in clarity, directness, and flexibility. I hope that poetry will be more and more written to be spoken or acted, and that it will become more and more part of the writer's function to learn to speak and read aloud, and, where necessary, to act. Even before I had done much broadcasting I found myself disinclined to write verse that was not meant to be read aloud or spoken.

It was my intention after the War to begin a novel which would commemorate a certain residuary and unstandardized way of living in a London sphere of which I had intimate knowledge before the War. Not being a tempestuous or regular novelist, I took my time over this book, with the result that I was able to shape it exactly as I wanted it. I worked within what I believed to be my proper scope, and intermittently, as the distractions of everyday life allowed. The book appeared under the title *Museum Pieces*. I have a special affection for it, and would not wish to alter a word or a comma. When I speak of distractions, I should perhaps explain that I have tended in life to give precedence to personal relationships, and there have been some which have seemed exacting, and agitating, and tedious all at the same time: but where I have had the belief, or the illusion, that my constancy was useful, pleasant, or necessary, I have not allowed it to lapse. A perhaps feminine side of my nature has in these instances taken charge. If I had lacked it, I suppose I might have more furiously and singlemindedly stuck to writing; but the pleasures and duties of human intercourse, to say nothing of the business of earning a living, have with me alternated with the lonely struggle of composing books. There has been this advantage, that I have not written against time to make money, and that everything I have written is related to everything else and to its originator. Such as it is, it is all of a piece.

17

A Friend Writes

BEFORE the War more space was given in *The Times* to obituary notices, especially to those supplementary ones sent in by friends of the deceased, than is given now. Real emotion is likely to be either eloquent or silent. If it finds expression in flat or trite phrases it seems, though it may not be, unreal. The prevalence of cant and cliché in these notices showed an almost total want of spontaneity and inventiveness. Again and again one read of *unremitting* labour or toil, of *consummate* tact, of *indefatigable* industry, of *unabated* zest, of *selfless* devotion, of *utter* unselfishness, of *inflexible* determination, of *deep* loyalties, of *long* experience, of *varied* responsibilities, of *indomitable* courage, of a *keen* sense of humour, of *infectious* laughter, of *sterling* integrity, of *conspicuous* success, of *untiring* energy, of *unfailing* generosity. Could it be believed of any human being that 'all children and animals worshipped him'? *All*? Or of another that 'he achieved instant popularity with everyone'? Or of another that 'he was loved by all'? Or of another that 'he was quite incapable of a mean thought'? Or of another that 'no one who met him could fail to be influenced by him'? Or of another that 'he had an immense affection for all animals'? Did he cherish wart-hogs and dote on hyenas? Did he take the skunk to his bosom?

The effort to prove that the deceased was a superman often took the form of saying that 'if ever there was a born soldier' — or 'saint on earth', or 'leader of men' — 'it was he'. Or, 'one felt instinctively that here was an individual of no ordinary mould'. There were many variations on the theme that the world would be 'the poorer for his passing' (surely an ambiguous statement), that 'his death has cast gloom over a wide circle', or that 'he has left a gap which can never be filled'. This last statement is hardly worth making, because it is true of every human being that dies. It was very refreshing to read, by contrast, about one man that 'he was a zealous beagler', and about another that 'of boomerangs he had a large collection'. There at least was something to remember him by.

'Is it not strange', asks Mr Forester in *Melincourt*, 'that even the fertility of fiction should be so circumscribed in the variety of monumental panegyric?'

'I have often thought', replies Mr Fox, 'that these words of Rabelais would furnish an appropriate inscription for ninety-nine gravestones out of every hundred: *Sa mémoire expira avecque le son des cloches qui carillonèrent à son enterrement.*'

Somewhere between the ostentatiously loyal friend and the painfully candid friend is the affectionate and understanding friend, and perhaps he can sometimes note down something more worth reading than banal generalities.

A number of the persons dear to me, admired by me, or well known to me, who had died during the War had not been killed by bombs or bullets, mines or torpedoes, but their deaths had evidently come sooner because of the anxiety, strain, fear, grief, gloom, and uncertainty about the future brought on by the War. As a disease of the body politic, war is felt in all its members. When more is understood about psychosomatic illnesses greater knowledge may help the doctor and the psychiatrist towards recognizing them and their causes, but hardly towards the prevention or cure of international catastrophes.

A Friend Writes

Of persons mentioned in this book, my mother had died in the first few weeks of the War. Nearing her last days, she was strangely haunted and evidently tormented by dreams and delirious visions of troop movements in Asia. She described them to me, and they proved strangely prophetic. The suffering that was to come to millions after she was dead seemed part of her own while she was still alive.

Just before she took to her deathbed, I went to see her one morning in the nursing home where she died. She was sitting by the window in a dressing gown, polishing her nails.

'If I'd known you were coming,' she said, 'I would have done this earlier. But I dare say you won't mind if I go on with it.' She looked up, and then said, in a lightly ironical tone of voice, 'After all, one has to do one's nails.'

Those were not her last words, but they would have done very well. They were wonderfully characteristic, mingling self-mockery, calmness, courage, and a kind of disdain for the world and for the last of the various traps in which her destiny had caught and wounded her; but, most of all, those words expressed her devotion to the order in which she believed and which her life had been a constant struggle to maintain against great and various odds.

Virginia Woolf was dead, a being not designed to withstand incorrigible barbarism, the ceaseless activity and energy of her word-shaping mind leaving behind her the trail of a comet, of which the luminosity will not be properly appreciated until the rest of what she wrote is printed. The ebullient but diabetic Hugh Walpole, whom she had so enjoyed teasing, was dead. He had served on the Russian front in the first War but was clearly neither young enough, strong enough, nor calm and balanced enough to withstand the second on the London front.

At Home

Anthony Butts's death had been doubly horrible, in its cause and in its details. To the very last he never lost his nerve. The freedom of his nature and his satirical high spirits had never diminished. He had foreseen in his twenties the disasters which a civilization in which he had lost confidence had brought upon itself. Born in 1900, a child of this century, he had thought, rightly or wrongly, that Europe had lost its way and that the benefits it had brought to Asia and Africa had been fatally outweighed by arrogance, exploitation, want of imagination, want of foresight, and puritanical materialism.

I thought of him in January, 1957, when a remarkable letter appeared in the *Spectator* from Mr J. C. Longhurst, with whose views he would have been likely to find himself in sympathy. 'Rather than glory in our past and continue to justify discrimination against those whose skins and ways of life are different from ours,' wrote Mr Longhurst, 'the present generation would be wise to try to earn their friendship; for theirs is the future, ours is the past.' Having worked among Chinese, Indians, and Negroes in various places, he had found that resentment and loathing, not liking or respect, was what Europeans most often incurred. It was not 'the Christian ethics of love and understanding' that had impressed them, but rather 'the history of killing and subjugation (interpreted in Europe as "keeping law and order" and "bringing civilization and industrial development") practised by most European nations ... throughout Africa and Asia'. And in his view 'the nemesis threatening Western Europeans, North Americans, and all other white skins, and even exceeding the threat of Communism, is that of revenge by the formerly subject lands of Asia and Africa for the cruelties and indignities endured by them in the past'.

I would not myself go so far as to say 'theirs is the future, ours

A Friend Writes

is the past,' though the decline of Europe's former expansive powers and conquering rapacity, and the rise of new expansiveness and rapacity in Asia and Africa have already altered the look of the world. But the concatenation of circumstances that fixed me when young in Asia and Africa made me acquainted with the wounds and anger of the insulted and oppressed; and my writings show, I believe, some consciousness of them. It is to me remarkable that I should have happened to live in South Africa, where the idea of white domination, raised by fanaticism to a matter of principle, is making its last, blind, unscrupulous stand; and in Japan, the first Asian nation to take over successfully the mechanical and industrial techniques of the West, the first in modern times to defeat a European Power in war, and the first to explode finally, by conquering and occupying colonial territories, any remaining illusion among Asian peoples of European invincibility. Japanese militarist imperialism proved no less odious than any other variety. Having foreseen its tendencies and probable consequences, and expressed my hatred of them, I was not surprised by them. And though I should not wish to try and excuse Japanese barbarities during the Second World War, it would not be senseless to try and perceive their causes, and to recognize among them a desire to avenge contempt shown towards the Japanese people by Europeans and Americans. Directly the War was over I resumed contact with my Japanese friends. If they were responsible for the maltreatment and murder of prisoners, I was no less responsible for the fate of Hiroshima. If the ties that bind individuals together are broken, what is left? Nothing but hopes of a better world or a better future, and better than hopes are handshakes.

Anthony Butts left behind him, besides cherished memories, a few paintings and the imperfect draft in typescript of a book he

had written with my encouragement. He hoped I would edit it
for publication. I did so, and it appeared in 1945, under the title
Curious Relations. It has entertained many readers on both sides of
the Atlantic. Some of them would be surprised to know how
much stranger than fiction are some of its apparently farfetched
characters and incidents. The book is a kind of satirical fantasia
solidly based upon fact. The genial verve of its author's disillusionment with the late Victorian and Edwardian society which had
evolved him and in which he grew up might blind a reader to its
significance as the work of a man who had found out that the
values of that society were false and wished to replace them with
other values.

Not very long after the War died Lilian Bowes Lyon. She, too,
was not satisfied with the values that her background and upbringing had seemed to require her to take for granted. But where
to Anthony Butts there had seemed a lack of vision on the part
of Europeans in regard to Asians and Africans, to her it seemed
that there was a want of vision in England about the genius of
the English people, which she believed to be partly warped or
thwarted by, chiefly, the poverty of a great part of them in her
time. If some of the intellectuals of the Thirties were sentimental
about the working class, some were uneasy and ashamed, where a
great mass of comfortable Philistines were indifferent or complacent, about unemployment and its consequences. I used to tease
her and call her a Bolshevik, but I am not sure that she was a
political being at all. She was not interested in the levelling down
of the more fortunate to the condition of the less fortunate, nor in
any kind of levelling at all. She was a poet with an acute response
to the creative stirrings, however blind or dumb, of every human
being.

Women who can no longer rely upon youth, or the resilience

of health, or the natural attractiveness that goes with both, or upon a settled social or family status, or upon the accepted claims of domestic responsibility, must still maintain their own being. In the effort to do so, they easily tend to become domineering; or, if they fail in that, to become discontented; and then, at the same time as they instinctively try to hide their frustration, they unconsciously draw attention to it, and grow cranky or grotesque. This may show in their appearance, manner, belief, or way of living, or some mingling of these, which may also be a mingling of the absurd, the disagreeable, and the pathetic. Of the least tinge of such grotesqueness Lilian Bowes Lyon remained utterly free. Too large a nature to impose upon others or to be sorry for herself, she felt a personal responsibility for the suffering of others. Her own physical anguish and her compassion for others seemed to eat her away like a double fire. In such a state she had chosen to go and live in Stepney and share the exposure of its people to the hazards of poverty and war. From time to time I was able to visit her there. Her concern with the lives around her seemed so different from that of those who used to go slumming that I asked her to try and put something down on paper about it. She did so, and what she wrote appeared pseudonymously in print, in the form of a letter addressed to myself.

She had always known, she said, that England was 'two nations' and had felt it to be wrong. This conviction had been fortified by her life in Stepney. She felt that even in peacetime it had only been their 'innate brotherliness, sanity, and grit' which had enabled the poor to stand up to life. She felt that, apart from actual want, poverty can so arrest development that people can be kept at what she called 'a psychological subsistence level', a condition in which 'the person nearly everybody could be, the hatched-out butterfly or imago, remains a chrysalis'. Deeply as I respect her longing for 'the natural burgeoning of body and mine,' her suspicion of the do-gooders and 'the Planners', her ability to be 'thankfully aware' of other people, and the stress she laid upon the importance of freedom and love being given to children, I could not altogether share her belief in the possibilities of beneficent change. Children, she felt rightly and strongly, must be given the chance to act their dreams. But when she suggested that 'a practical way to help the imago in the great mass of our fellow countrymen' would be to let them make manifest their dreams and aspirations, I felt a little out of my depth, and began to tease her again. They needed security, she said, to give them scope; they needed 'freedom to become'. Yes, but—scope for what? to become what? If by chance dreams and aspirations are base or cheap or noxious, is it so desirable for them to be made manifest? And what degree of 'security' is desirable? In countries with a high level of social security—Sweden, for example—has there been no increase in boredom, no weakening of 'sanity and grit', and of those fibres of character which insecurity can toughen?

Whatever the answers to those questions, the wisdom or logic of her arguments seemed to me far less important than the glow, the warmth, the generosity of her feelings. She had a rare sense of the potential creative power of 'ordinary' people, a respect for them and love for them, and a wish to share her own vision with them, to which they quickly and no less warmly responded. 'East Ends, wherever they may be,' she wrote, '. . . should be seen not primarily with the objective eye but as Blake perhaps would see them if he were alive today, in terms of pity and terror and the mighty rushing wind of inspiration.' In short, there was nothing prosaic about the inhabitants of *her* East End.

A Friend Writes

I have known and admired a good many poets. It ought not to be necessary to say that their lives are conditioned by the needs of their poetry. It may not be easy always to see the point of their irregular lives, to agree with their unreasonable views, to sympathize with their obsessive fantasies and stupid prejudices, to regard as seriously as they do the attitudes they assume, but these things are part of the medium in which alone they may be able to function, or of the apparatus that enables them to function. A duchess whose devotion to poetry seemed wholehearted, and who herself wrote poetry, complained to me of a poet whom we both knew that his nails were dirty: I could not help saying that we both knew a great many people with clean nails who could not write poetry. Lilian Bowes Lyon did not happen to belong to the dirty nail school, but in her own way was as much agitated by ideas of social change as some other poets of the thirties. Whatever their limitations, their tendencies were prophetic of the social revolution that has since taken place.

When friends die, part of oneself seems torn away, but really they have added a cell to that transitory agglomeration of cells that is oneself, enabling one to reflect life, to reflect about life, and to live more fully than before. And if they have had some power with the written word, that is something specially personal to remember them by. I did not feel able to write the introduction to Lilian Bowes Lyon's *Collected Poems*, which fortunately appeared in time for her to see them. It was admirably done by Cecil Day Lewis: I had introduced them to one another in Gloucestershire about fifteen years earlier. 'More rigorously, more devotedly, more intimately than most poets of our time,' he wrote, 'Lilian Bowes Lyon has identified herself with suffering humanity.' He perceived the depth and the darkness in her writings, and the note of passion which he felt Christina Rossetti and Emily Brontë would have recognized. And he quoted some lines that I too have found memorable, for instance:

> So chary of breath
> Each alien burr
> Clings light to earth,
> Foredoomed to thaw.
> Sigh and they are gone,
> Like snow bees following sweetness;
> The ghostly are blown,
> Are chosen away to brightness.

And,

> Some covet life to lose it; some agree
> With Christ at last, like dew the sun draws up.

I myself am haunted besides by the following lines:

> And where, too, martyrs lie after long suffering,
> Drained all of anger's colour, blank as snow
> In the shadeless dream of their achieved self-offering,
> Ask that for these may blow
> The hot south rage of life again, up-levering,
> To stand erect, a choir of close-knit bones.

'In nature,' Chekhov once said, 'a repulsive caterpillar turns into a lovely butterfly. But with human beings it's the other way round: a lovely butterfly turns into a repulsive caterpillar.' That is a doctor's-eye view. To a doctor the physical and psychological habits, the flabby tissues and shabby complainings of the ageing must always seem a gross degeneration from the clean-eyed pliancy of the young. But often the characters of the sick and dying have seemed to me to be stepping like heroic figures out of the beggarly trappings of mortality, the sentence of death having smoothed away from their mental lineaments what was mean or trivial.

Another poet whom I knew, Demetrios Capetanakis, who died young in 1944, had the rare distinction of finding himself able to write in English although it was not his mother tongue. It is gratifying that so learned and subtle a mind should have found English 'the poetic language par excellence'. Dame Edith Sitwell, in an essay published after his death, spoke of the strangeness, wisdom, and profundity of his poetry, and of his mastery of English. I was greatly interested in his feelings about England and the English, and wrote after his death: 'We of the north and the west turn towards the sun; we look to the south and the east and the past for beauty and strangeness; we have looked with curiosity and passion to the Mediterranean, our Goethes and Byrons to Italy and Greece, our Flauberts to Carthage, our Gissings to Rome; we have looked to the Arab countries and towards Asia for the unknown and the exotic, the strangely stirring. But Demetrios in the lucid aridity of Greece had dreamt of the north and the west and the present, the blond energies of the German, the Englishman dreaming and smiling in his fogs, the fantastic activity of the American'.* Drawn to the dampness and darkness of England and the Dickensian aspects of London, and fascinated by its febrile atmosphere in the nightly blackout of wartime, he had discovered that the English were the gentlest and the most stubborn people in the world—gentle and stubborn at the same time, because neither too gentle nor

* From "A Recollection" in *Demetrios Capetanakis: A Greek Poet in England*, edited and published by John Lehmann in 1947.

too stubborn. 'Balance', he wrote, 'is the secret of the English genius', and the English language could express the light as well as the darkness of the soul, he found, with equal power. By his discovery of England he helped me to understand my own.

18

If I Were Doctor Gruber

SUPPOSE I were in fact Dr Gruber. What kind of England
might I have discovered? Let us postulate a man just turned
thirty, settling in England in the early Thirties for politico-
racial reasons and in the hope of pursuing his career and bringing
up a family in comparative security. One of my great-grand-
fathers was a country doctor at Frome in Somerset in the time of
William IV, and when he died, in the early eighteen-forties, the
tradesmen shut up their shops and pulled down their blinds—
which is more than they would do today. I like to think of Dr
Gruber as living, but as a man who would be worth pulling one's
blinds down for if the occasion arose; a humane and tolerant man
with high standards of professional conduct, with medical and
psychological curiosity and powers of observation, and a readiness for varied experience.

It is not unlikely that when Dr Gruber first came to England he
had formed some general opinion about the English, or had
accepted it ready-made. He would have heard that the English
are cold and reserved, stolid and unemotional, mad, hypocritical,
lazy, dull, either indifferent or hostile towards foreigners, class
conscious, obsessed with ball games, dog addicts, and cherishers
of all sorts of archaic survivals. But being a cultivated man, he
will naturally have distrusted generalizations about national
character. He will have known that the English are a mixed and
mongrel race, and have expected to find among them every sort of

contradiction and variety. His expectation will not have been disappointed.

He will never, I daresay, have quite got over the discovery that the English are in general not merely unemotional but incapable of emotion, let alone passion. Their pudding faces are not masks, but the surfaces of puddings that are puddings all through. . . . But are they? The question will often have posed itself, because he will have noticed evidence of gentleness and stubbornness, and these are not attributes of the pudding. If there have been moments when he has agreed with John Stuart Mill about 'the general meanness of English life', about 'the low objects on which the faculties of all classes of the English are intent', and about the way in which their feelings and intellectual faculties remain undeveloped, so that passion is incomprehensible to them and intellectuality absurd, he will have found this picture reversible. Inclined at first to think the tameness and dullness of English life boring—its brief exchanges of formulae about the weather seeming, for example, a sad change from the copious exchange of ideas in cafés—he may have begun to perceive that it is restful. He may have learnt that it allows an unusual degree of freedom to the individual and to the workings of his mind and conscience—if any. He will have noticed that there is less likelihood here of riot, massacre, and assassination than in some other countries. The Englishman's want of excitability, his disinclination for scenes, his common inability to be easily or badly rattled, are indicated by his habit of understatement, just as his distaste for boasting finds expression in self-depreciation: to Dr Gruber these will not be signs of stupidity, but signs of a reserve of strength. As a doctor he will soon have seen that the Englishman's habit of not working frantically hard saves him from the nervous and physical tension that often afflicts those who do. The Englishman's stolidity he is likely to have found inseparable from a formidable tenacity, and the Englishman's reserve sometimes only preoccupation, broodiness, or shyness, and often a mask for kindliness.

After a varied experience of English life in many aspects, and having for a time carried on his practice in urban environments, Dr Gruber will know that some of the conditions he has found, whether physical or mental, are not specifically English, but are due to the pressures of overpopulation in any industrial environment in the twentieth century. He will have noticed a progressive standardization of behaviour, a degeneration of individuality, and a want of taste and inventiveness in everyday life, in food, clothes, and furniture—but not in mechanical and applied science. He will inevitably have found the English in many ways a dirty people. He will remember having read in the report for 1955 of the chief medical officer of the Ministry of Education that a quarter of a million children were found with verminous heads. He will have noticed uncleanness for which poverty is not accountable. He will have visited patients in dirty habitations, and patients will have exposed dirty bodies to him in his own consulting rooms. The goatish armpits of a waitress, the scarlet-painted but filthy nails of a bus conductress, the expectorations of some oafish pipe smoker, dirty feet, the grime and litter of railways, streets, parks, beaches, and other public resorts will have obtruded themselves upon his senses. And, knowing that it is a human failing to accuse others of our own failings, he will hardly have been surprised to hear, for example, contemptuous allusions to 'dirty Wogs' or 'Gyppoes'. Not easily shocked, he will have been shocked by instances of cruelty to children, of a kind seldom or never heard of among races regarded as inferior. The Teutonic love of uniforms, and of leagues, and of patriotic or military rituals and routines will have saddened him; and as a doctor, dedicated to the preservation of life, he must particularly have noticed the daily massacre on the roads and the callousness of many of its perpetrators: but this, like dishonesty, or meanness, or insolence, he will certainly not have considered peculiar to this island.

Reading (again in Mill) about 'the error always prevalent in England . . . of judging universal questions by a merely English standard', he will have marked this phrase (methodically trained and methodically minded man that he is) with a line in the margin. And it will have led him to reflect (not for the first time, and so far as his professional duties have allowed) on the whole question of the English attitude to the non-English—a question with which he has inevitably been a good deal concerned. Though not politically minded, his residence in England will have caused him to reflect a little upon the rise and decline of the British Empire. He will remember one of his compatriots, who had been at school in England, recalling how the expression 'law and order' seemed like one word—*lawnorder*—and was at first believed by him to show some connection between the pax Britannica and the well-kept patch of grass in the Englishman's garden. Sometimes, noticing the expression 'law and order' in some newspaper or radio report, Dr Gruber may have meditated over Europe's expansive past. Where other nations have sometimes been far more oppressive and unjust, and have not always provided anything like the same framework of roads, schools, hospitals, law courts, and cricket fields, the English, to him, may seem to have been—and still at times to be—too heavyhanded in their determination to impose *lawnorder* upon peoples of quite different temper and aspirations to their own. A phrase like 'judging it necessary to impose (or maintain) *lawnorder*', issuing from administrative lips or rattled out on pedagogic typewriters, may have seemed to him to have meant to those upon whom *lawnorder* was imposed a cold and arrogant disregard of what they passionately believed to be their rights and knew to be their ethnic or religious traditions, an indifference towards their familiar habits of mind, and a disdain for their customary ebullitions of temperament. It may have seemed to him that when these supposed rights, accepted ways, and usual vagaries did not conform with those of the English, *lawnorder* might prove to mean not tidiness and decency but force, punishment, and war, where a little more imagination might conceivably have led to compromise, partnership, and mutual loyalty. Ireland and South Africa may have seemed to him examples where a long persistence of rapacity, shortsightedness, and military extravagance ended in retreat and moral defeat as well.

Like others of English domicile but not of English origin, Dr Gruber can hardly have ignored the existence of xenophobia among the English. He may have heard the word 'foreigner' used as disparagingly as the words 'nigger', 'Kaffir', or 'Jew' are used in various parts of the world. He may at times have longed to point out that to most of the human race an Englishman is a foreigner. I myself learnt this fact in many different ways when young. Once in my early twenties, for instance, I was walking through a village in the Japanese Alps. 'A foreigner, a foreigner!' I heard the people calling out to one another, and the whole village, dogs included, turned out and ran after me in great excitement. I was told that they had never seen a European before and that I was probably the first who had ever set foot in the place. Those villagers belonged to one of the many nations who have held the belief that they were of divine origin, a chosen race with a special destiny and a civilization that set them above all others.

At Home

My presence may have seemed like a vague threat to their security, and the fear that somebody from outside is endangering the inside may be ancient and primitive but is often well founded. It is closely linked with the notion that an outsider must be inferior.

I once knew a military man who had a violent prejudice, of personal and childish origin, against the French. As he was certainly part of the backbone of this country I will call him Major Vertebra. His prejudice had cut him off from one of the great sources of our civilization; he professed to believe that the French were good for nothing—politically, militarily, collectively, and individually. But even in his own country his peace of mind was threatened by outsiders. The poor man was once heard to say, not humorously, not in a moment of exasperation, but in deadly earnest, 'I must say *I can't stand civilians*! I can't make them out at all!'

If that was what he felt about the greater number of his fellow countrymen, including his wife (if not uniformed) and his mother (if he ever had one), no wonder he was contemptuous about all those lesser breeds who, in his view, so obviously began at Calais and extended all over the globe—dirty, excitable, unreliable, and equally contemptible whether civilians or aspiring to military ascendancy. He was the kind of man who is provoked by some item of news into exclaiming, 'I can't stand the Babylonians!' or 'The only good Visigoth is a dead Visigoth!' He was as much a disseminator of nonsense as those foreigners who assert that all the English are cold, arrogant, and perfidious; or as some Arab who believes that all Westerners are rich; or some knowing Asian who explains that all Europeans are hairy, and that intimate physical contact with them (except for money) is best avoided because they smell like camels or like corpses.

The distaste with which Major Vertebra would regard Dr

If I Were Doctor Gruber

Gruber is easily imaginable. He would resent him as a Jew, as an intellectual, and as an outsider. It would not have occurred to him that there are particular reasons why in this island we should be careful what we say about outsiders—chiefly that a variety of them went to the making of us. We are, thank goodness, a mixed race. The idea of pure breeding has its place on the farm, in the kennel or in the sty, but since Hitler the thought of it among human beings is not easily acceptable. A few years ago a physicist, Dr Furth, addressing the British Association at Edinburgh, gave it as his view that the formation of what might be called 'pure communities' of people belonging to the same race—whatever that meant—was dangerous for the maintenance of democracy. He felt that to establish a stable human society it was necessary to allow a certain amount of mixing of populations. He recalled some of the things that have been done with a view to strengthening social or national communities, or expelling minorities—things like segregating different races within a community, or expelling minorities—and he pointed out how these things had produced an exactly opposite effect to what was intended.

The English tradition of admitting foreign refugees from political, racial, or religious persecutions is sound and sensible. When they choose to stay here, to learn our different language and acclimatize themselves to our complex and, to them, foreign ways, they will not be pleased to hear themselves spoken of as 'bloody foreigners': by their lives and work they are contributing to our lives and our work, and their temperaments, like their special skills, must diversify and enrich the texture of English life. Doctor Gruber (as I imagine him) and I have more in common than our appearance. I conceive of him as having settled in this country, and I have done the same myself. Where he must regard himself, though naturalized, as an exile, I find myself fortunately conscious of roots and background and affinities, and at home. But our reasons for staying here may be to some extent the same. English gentleness, English stubbornness, English well-meaningness, English balance and tolerance, the English disinclination to panic or boasting, English stoicism, many graces, something in the atmosphere—these we find worth living with and worth living for. Affection and habit deepen into love and loyalty, and occasions of agreement are made fruitful by the still inalienable right to differ.

I wonder if Dr Gruber sometimes thinks, as I do, of the deformity of the England we have lived in, and of the France we have visited. It has been at best a mutilated civilization we have known, a makeshift, because it has had to do without those who were killed between 1914 and 1918. The enormity of that loss, the destruction of such an inestimable treasure of heart and head, is not to be imagined. By me, at least, it is never long forgotten. I tend to think of the boyish Euseby Beecher, a young assistant master at my preparatory school near Sevenoaks. I remember rides on the back of his motor bicycle and his supple waist between my hands. I remember his talent for drawing, and his enigmatic smile. Nature expends much to save little, but I am no more reconciled to his death, or persuaded that it was necessary, than I am to the death of Wilfred Owen and all those slaughtered contemporaries of many nations. Perhaps after all the greatest thing said in those days was that 'Patriotism is not enough'. It took a woman to say that.

I have felt no compulsion to return to Asia or Africa. More than once I have declined invitations to take up positions in Japan. I know that I have left more than a fiftieth part of myself there, I know that part of me is part of Japan, but I do not yet feel that this cross-grafting process must be repeated. As for South Africa,

since the Twenties I have had no relations there except dead ones
— my infant brother John, buried at Louis Trichardt half a century
ago, and 'poor Uncle Durham who was killed in the War'. I had
neither friends, nor ambitions, nor purpose, nor property, to
draw me back there. I remembered Africa as a complex and
violent revelation made to me when young. From all that I knew,
its complexity and violence had increased: I could not imagine
living there in a state of tension that I should only find endurable
if bent upon martyrdom or at least victimization.

Twelve years after the Second World War I did revisit South
Africa, in response to an invitation from the University of the
Witwatersrand, than which I am older. I had not seen Africa for
thirty years, and so learnt what it must be like to return as a ghost
to scenes of former life. The account of my haunting of those
scenes does not belong here. I will allude instead to a ghost that
haunts me—the ghost of an African woman. In the summer of
1862 a Mrs Price, the wife of a missionary, arrived one evening
with her husband at Mashuwe in Bechuanaland. Under a tree
they saw a creature lying. It was a human being. It was female.
At the approach of the white strangers she rose and gazed wonder-
ingly at them. If she had not risen to her feet, she might have been
presumed dead. She was a living skeleton—and yet parts of her
body were 'bloated and swollen with virulent smallpox'. One of
her hands was huge and shapeless, and blood was oozing from a
wound in her face. Her breasts were full, like those of a nursing
mother. In her diseased condition and a very advanced state of
pregnancy she had been driven from home by her mother and
husband. She had taken refuge under this tree alone, and the day
before the Prices arrived had given birth, unaided, to her child.
In the night she was attacked by a hyena, which dragged her
baby from her arms and devoured it. After a time the hyena came

back and attacked her, causing the wound that Mrs Price saw, but she had somehow managed to defend herself from being killed by it.

This hellish happening * has fixed itself in my mind as an image of Africa, almost as clearly as if it were a memory. It is easy enough to remember the wrongs of Europe's incursions into Africa — the slave trade, commercial exploitation, racial contempt, and social injustice: but it is as well to remember that the wrongs done by Africans to Africans, out of greed, cruelty, callousness, superstition, and ignorance, are beyond computing. What seems to me now far more worth remembering is all that has made less likely the solitude of that woman under the tree — compassion, charity, disinfectants, education, art, literature, even a measure of *lawn-order*; the idea of personal responsibility; the lives given to understanding, to forgiveness, to moral and material betterment; the scope given to pleasure and playfulness; the grounds given for hope.

In my early writings about South Africa and Japan it was plainly stated or implied that both were heading for trouble. In one country racialism was undermining the hope of unity, in the other militarist nationalism was preparing national disaster in a more impetuous way. But I was not a preacher or a political agitator, merely a youthful sensibility exposed to conditions of growing violence and falsehood and driven by a myth-making, image-making, character-drawing faculty to put these things in words, to try and shape them in prose and verse. The current doctrine that a writer has to be engaged with the problems of his time does not seem to have much novelty if one has had to live from an early age among the tensions created by 'problems'. But

---

* Described in the entry for 21st November, 1862, in *The Journals of Elizabeth Lees Price*, edited by Una Long (Edward Arnold).

If I Were Doctor Gruber

if I have since felt myself more widely and deeply engaged—with human nature, with the past, with the arts, with the battle against the cheapening and levelling of what is rare and diverse, and of life itself—this has been chiefly made possible for me by England, by English civilization, and by English men, women, and children.

Index

Index

Index

Index

Index